FUNDAMENTAL THEORIES OF ETHNIC CONFLICT

Explaining the root causes of ethnic and racial hate

Edited by
Muli Wa Kyendo

First printed and published in Kenya in 2019 by:

The Syokimau Cultural Centre,
P.O Box 20257-00100 Nairobi, Kenya.
Email: emmamuli@yahoo.com
Phone: (+254) 727536174, 721302418, 773991820

Copyright: Syokimau Cultural Centre 2019

ISBN 978-9966-7020-6-7

Design: Mutua Muli

Also available at:

African Books Collective
P.O. Box 721
Oxford, OXON OX1 9EN
United Kingdom
Email: orders@africanbookscollective.com

Amazon: http://bit.ly/mKyendoBooks

CONTENTS

PREFACE

FundamentalPrinciple

If you want to solve a problem, you must know what the problem is. It can be said that a large part of the solution lies in knowing what it is you are trying to do.

Theory is an essential tool in the scientific effort to predict and explain phenomena. It is useful in designing and planning effective strategies for intervention programs. It provides the foundation for selecting projects and tools with a better than random probability of success. In his book, *Preface to Logic*, Morris Cohen says that without some guiding idea we cannot determine what facts are relevant to the problem solution we are seeking.Concurring with this, Fred Kerlinger makes a fundamental principle: 'If one wants to solve a problem, one must generally know what the problem is. It can be said that a large part of the solution lies in knowing what it is one is trying to do."

In line with the above ideas, this book, as its title implies, concerns itself with developing and expanding on theories that aim at explaining the fundamental causes of ethnic and racial conflicts. It therefore, doesn't concern itself with the "effects theories" which deal with the consequences of ethnic and racial conflicts. The aim is to shift focus from research, policies and strategies based on tackling the effects of ethnic and racial conflicts, which have so far been ineffective as evidenced by the increase in ethnic conflicts, to more fundamental ideas, models and strategies. The variety of theories in this book will provide options that can assist in designing effective ethnic and racial peace promotion programs.

The book was inspired by the conditions in my country, Kenya, where ethnic violence erupted with terrifying consequences following a disputed election held in December 2007. According to official estimates, more than 1,400 people were brutally murdered while thousands of others were maimed or left homeless. In Eldoret, a multiethnic town in the Rift Valley, for example, hundreds of people including innocent children, were killed when a church into which over 1,500 people had fled to seek shelter, was torched. Joseph Kwasila, one of the people sheltering in the church who escaped death, told a newspaper reporter:

"I saw them burn it! We ran away and they chased us to the main road. They were like lions in a rage, with sticks and machetes".

The cruelty of the execution so shocked Kenyans and the world, that soon, everyone was expressing fears that the country was headed for a genocide in a scale similar to that which occurred in Rwanda in1994. Here is a descriptive newspaper report:

The armed men then slammed the church doors shut. They piled bicycles and mattresses outside the main entrance and blocked a smaller door at the back. They went about their business efficiently. Inside the small Kenya Assemblies of God Church in Kiambaa, just outside the town of Eldoret in western Kenya, dozens of terrified people huddled together. They were Kikuyus, members of the tribe that has borne the brunt of the violence that followed last week's disputed presidential election.

The attackers, members of the rival Kalenjin tribe, poured fuel on the mattresses and piled on dried maize leaves from a nearby field. Then they set the barricades alight and waited until the flames burned high. The church turned into an oven.

Traumatized Kenyans, including the then Chief Justice Dr. Willy Mutunga, came out calling for "profound, radical, and sustainable transformation" – a transformation that would fundamentally alter the very nature of "our vision and perception" as a people and a nation. As one person put it,

The task ahead (of Kenyans) requires courage to challenge basic assumptions and lifelong traditions. It demands boldness to place major bets on new ideas, models, and strategies that can bring peace to our country.

This book, I hope, will make useful contribution in this direction. It is planned to be particularly useful to policy makers, NGOs and others involved in creating peace. It will also be useful in guiding research and as text book in universities and colleges. Contents extend across many disciplines including evolution, biology, religion, communication, mythology and even introspective perspectives.

Drawn from around the world, contributors to the book are experienced, award winning authors, scholars and thinkers with deep understanding of their special fields of contribution. My very deep gratitude goes to them all for accepting the challenge to contribute their time, knowledge and ideas that may help to create a better and more peaceful world.

THE AUTHORS

Gary R. Johnson is a political scientist who studies the evolutionary origins of government, politics, and patriotism, as well as the broader field of politics and the life sciences. He is author of numerous articles and essays in this field, and has given numerous presentations and guest lectures on the subject. He served as Editor of *Politics and the Life Sciences* for ten years, as Executive Director of the Association for Politics and the Life Sciences for five years, and as President of the Michigan Political Science Association. In recognition of his professional service, he has received awards or honors from the Michigan Political Science Association, the Association for Politics and the Life Sciences, and the Arrowhead Model United Nations Association. Dr. Johnson is Professor Emeritus of Political Science at Lake Superior State University, Sault Ste. Marie, Michigan, USA, where—among other roles—he was the long-time chair of the Political Science Department. He is a recipient of university's Distinguished Teacher Award, as well as six awards for academic advising. He is currently working on an overview book on the evolutionary origins of government and politics. He may be contacted at GJOHNSON@LSSU.EDU.

Robert Sapolsky is John A. and Cynthia Fry Gunn Professor of biology at Stanford University, and of neurology and neurosurgery at Stanford University School of Medicine. He is also a research associate at the Institute of Primate Research, National Museums of Kenya. For many decades, Sapolsky has divided his time between the laboratory and field biology. The former has involved research on the effects of stress and stress hormones on the brain, and the use of gene therapy strategies to protect the nervous system from the damaging effects of stress. The field work has consisted of annual studies of populations of wild baboons living in the Serengeti Ecosystem of East Africa, examining the effects of rank, personality and social affiliation on patterns of stress-related disease. Sapolsky has authored numerous books for non-scientists, including *Why Zebras Don't Get Ulcers: A Guide to Stress, Stress-Related Disease and Coping* (3rd edition, 2004, Henry Holt); *A Primate's Memoir* (2001, Scribner) and *Behave: The Biology of Humans at Our Best and Worst* (2017, Penguin Books). A native of New York City, Sapolsky received his undergraduate education at Harvard University, and his PhD from Rockefeller University; he lives with his wife and children in San Francisco.

Dr. Glen T. Martin, is professor of philosophy at Radford University, USA and Chairperson of the university's Program in Peace Studies. As world citizen he has worked in service of world peace with justice for many years, travelling and lecturing in many countries and authoring many books. Martin is President of International Philosophers for Peace, President of the institute of World Problems and President of the World Constitution and Parliament Association. He has received many international awards as a result of his peace activities. They include The Gusi Peace Prize, ISISAR Global Peace Award, the World Peace Award, the Lighthouse of the World Award. He has also been nominated for Mahatma Gandhi Peace Award and the Prince of Asturias Award for Peace. His books include, *Millennium Dawn: the Philosophy of Planetary Crisis and Human Liberation (2005), Ascent to World Law (2008), Triumph of Civilization: Democracy, Non-violence* and *the Piloting of Spaceship Earth (2010), The Anatomy of a Sustainable World:: Our Choice between Climate Change or System Change (2013)* and *One World Reborn: Holistic Planetary Transformation through a Global Social Contract (2016).*

Bruce L. Cook Ph.D, is founder and Vice President of Worldwide Peace Organization, Vice President for Publicity, International Organization for World Peace and President of Global Harmony Organization—USA. He has devoted much of his time teaching at universities, researching, writing and promoting peace. Bruce has a B.A. in Radio-Television from Ohio Wesleyan University, an M.A. in Speech Arts from San Diego State University, and a Ph.D. in Communication from Temple University. He has authored and edited many publications including "Effectively Teaching Stressed-out Students" in *Promoting Global Peace and Civic Engagement through Education, Harmony of Nations, Strategies for Peace* and *Handbook of Research on Examining Global Peacemaking in the Digital Age.*

Harold W. Becker is the author of several books including, *Internal Power: Seven Doorways to Self Discovery, Unconditional Love – An Unlimited Way of Being,* and *Unconditional Love Is....* He holds an MBA from the University of Tampa and since 1990 has devoted his energy to help individuals and communities raise the awareness of humanity through his consulting company, Internal Insights. In 2000 he founded and is President of the internationally involved nonprofit organization, The Love Foundation, Inc., with the vision of "inspiring people to love unconditionally." He also founded Global Love Day for May 1st each year. Harold shares his powerful understanding about life through books, speaking, radio and television guest appearances, workshops, PBS television special, and through various social media channels. He currently resides in Orlando, Florida. He may be contacted at: John T. Goltz via email: jtgoltz@ internalinsights.com.

Muli Wa Kyendo has extensively studied the role of myths, legends and folktales in ethnic and racial conflicts. His Myth Values theory was first published as *Interethnic Conflicts: Understanding the Important Role of Folktales* in *Handbook of Research on Examining Global Peacemaking in the Digital Age.* He also discusses the same topic in a chapter titled, A Movement for Social Change? in *Strategies for Peace.* His acclaimed book on ethnic harmony, *Kioko and the Legend of the Plains,* has been described as, "a tale that is steeped in culture, that illustrates a beautiful setting, and that shows how two cultures who previously thought they were enemies can live in harmony". He is the founder and Director of the Syokimau Cultural Centre which works with folktales, myths and legends to bring about positive change in individuals and communities. Journalist, author and scholar, Muli read sociology at the University of Nairobi, Kenya and at the Free University in Berlin before training as a journalist. He has taught communication in universities and colleges. His latest book is the *Crows Will Tell: A collection of ngewa - fables - from the Akamba of Kenya (2017).*

THE ROOTS OF ETHNIC CONFLICT: AN EVOLUTIONARY PERSPECTIVE

Gary R. Johnson

Inherited Traits

Conflicts are the variable and proximate means by which individuals pursue their ultimate interest - maximizing the reproductive rate of the genes.

Over the last century alone, tens of millions of people have lost their lives in ethnic conflicts. Countless others have lost limbs, lost homes, lost livelihoods, or lost loved ones. Ethnic conflict is surely one of the contemporary world's most notable phenomena. Despite some special features associated with the rise of large-scale territorial states, however, this sanguinary phenomenon is not new. Indeed, we have good reasons, both empirical and theoretical, to believe that ethnic conflict is an ancient phenomenon and that its roots lie deep in human nature.

This chapter examines the evolutionary roots of ethnic conflict. I approach this task with considerable humility. In the first place, there is already a rich descriptive and analytical literature on ethnic conflict by erudite scholars who have devoted most of their professional lives to this subject (e.g., Horowitz 1985; Connor 1994). I do not presume to speak with this kind of substantive expertise. On the other hand, the existing theoretical framework for explaining ethnic conflict is rudimentary, at best. It is here that an outsider may be able to make some contribution - not on the basis of wide or deep knowledge of the subject - but by bringing a different perspective.

Second, this is not the first attempt to examine the evolutionary roots of ethnic conflict. Pierre van den Berghe's excellent *The Ethnic Phenomenon* (1981; see also Salter 2001) holds pride of place there, and others have contributed additional insights (including the contributors to Reynolds, Falger, and Vine 1987; Ross 1981, 1991; Shaw and Wong 1989; Warnecke, Masters, and Kempter 1992; Fox 1994). Nevertheless, the application of evolutionary theory to the study of human behavior is still in its infancy. Pioneering work may need to be extended and refined, and in some cases amended. Moreover, no scientific theory is ever final and complete. Indeed, the best that any scientifically oriented analyst can hope for is to make some useful (and contingent) contribution to the ongoing collective effort of advancing scientific understanding.

An examination of a phenomenon's evolutionary roots might reasonably begin by defining the phenomenon and then working backward to its roots. It may be more useful in this case, however, to begin with the roots of conflict itself and then work forward, attempting to generate the phenomena we refer to as "ethnic conflict." I will begin, therefore, with an analysis of the origins of conflict. I will then proceed to examine the roots of cooperation, the mechanisms through which allies and enemies are recognized, and the ways in which these mechanisms may have been manipulated to allow humans to build larger alliances, including those we refer to as ethnic groups. This leads me, finally, to reexamine, from this evolutionary perspective, a number of important issues regarding our understanding of ethnic conflict.

The Roots of Conflict

Assumptions about the nature and origin of conflict are fundamental to virtually all theories of human behavior. Evolutionary theory suggests - by contrast with both Marxist theory and many standard social science accounts - that there are conflicts of interest among all humans. This is because the ultimate (or distal) interest of any organism is its genetic fitness. It is genes that are transmitted across generations, and genes are therefore the ultimate currency in natural selection. From this perspective, the observable objects of humans conflicts - territory, property, resources, power, privilege, wealth, security, status - are not ends in themselves. They are, instead, the variable and proximate means by which individuals pursue their ultimate interest - maximizing the reproductive rate of the genes they carry (Dawkins 1976, 1982; Alexander 1987).

These inherent, genotypic conflicts of interest are grounded in sexual reproduction. In contrast to asexual organisms, which (ignoring mutations) produce genetically identical daughter cells, humans and other sexually-reproducing organisms produce offspring that carry only a proportion of each parent's genes (50% for humans and most other sexually-reproducing species). Every human, then, with the exception of monozygotic twins, is genetically unique. Sexual reproduction, therefore, by its very nature, produces individuals who have conflicting genetic interests (Alexander 1979, 1987). This is true even of parents and offspring. Parents and offspring share substantial genetic interests, but since offspring are related to each parent by a factor of only .5, there are also substantial conflicts of genetic interest between them. These conflicts manifest themselves in a variety of ways, depending upon the species and its ecological circumstances, but they are always present in a sexually reproducing species (Trivers 1974).

Given the nature of sexual reproduction, then, conflict would be expected among all individuals except monozygotic twins. And we can expect conflict even among these rare exceptions to genetic uniqueness. First, since monozygotic twins may actually differ slightly because of mutations that occur during cell division, even they may have slightly conflicting genetic interests. Second - and even if they were truly identical - we must remember that monozygotic twins are relatively uncommon. Since evolution produces proximate mechanisms to serve ultimate (distal) ends, and since these proximate mechanisms evolve on the basis of statistically normal conditions, genetically identical organisms in a sexually-reproducing species will not "know" that their interests are identical. Their behavior-generating mechanisms evolved under conditions in which virtually every other conspecific was at least a partial genetic competitor. For this reason, monozygotic twins will come into conflict despite their genetic identity. Consequently, we may assert that conflicts of interest exist among all members of a sexually-reproducing species. This would certainly include those who are bonded together in ethnic groups. Shared ethnicity, therefore, is no guarantee of cooperation and amity.

The Roots of Cooperation

Conflicts of interest may be ubiquitous in a Darwinian world, but that is not necessarily a recipe for a Hobbesian war of all against all. Effective competition need not be a solitary enterprise. Organisms often compete more effectively by collaborating with other organisms. Competition with some is suspended, restricted, or rechanneled in order to more effectively compete with others (whether of one's own or a different species).

When such cooperation assumes regular, complex patterns over extended periods of time, new kinds of units are created. Thus, all complex organisms, as well as the cells of which those organisms are composed, are products of enduring patterns of cooperation among lower-level units. Among humans, such relatively enduring alliances become families, clans, businesses, professional associations, and whole societies. The collectivities we refer to as "ethnic groups" have the potential to become such an enduring alliance; when they do, they have become a "nation."

Ignoring for now the possibility of group selection, all cooperation appears to be built on one or more of three foundations: nepotism, reciprocity, and exploitation. Most complex instances of cooperation probably involve a complicated mix of all three. Nevertheless, it is important to distinguish among these three foundations of cooperation.

Nepotism, of course, is favorable treatment of kin. This route to social collaboration is a product of kin selection, a type of natural selection in which gene frequencies in a subsequent generation are influenced by the effects of the behavior of an individual on the reproduction of relatives, either lineal or collateral (Hamilton 1964; Maynard Smith 1964, 1976). Kin selection can produce cooperation and altruism among relatives because relatives share genes.

Cooperation with a relative - even life-sacrificing altruism - may therefore enhance the reproduction of these shared genes. At the genetic level, these behaviors are competitive and egoistic - they enhance the individual's genetic interest. At the phenotypic level, however, these same behaviors are cooperative and altruistic (Alexander 1974, 1979; Dawkins 1976).

The most obvious example of phenotypic altruistic behavior is parental care. Parental care entails phenotypic sacrifice by the parent (for example, in energy expended and danger encountered in gathering food for offspring). Parents may even sacrifice their lives for their offspring. Nevertheless, it has always been easy to understand how such behavior on behalf of offspring could be established by natural selection. What was not so easy to understand, at least until William Hamilton's path breaking analysis in 1964, was that this same logic applies to collateral as well as lineal relatives. Hamilton recognized that the evolutionary foundation of parental behavior is shared genes, and that such sharing of genes applies to relatives other than offspring, even if in reduced proportions.

Hamilton demonstrated that the probability of altruistic behavior being directed toward a conspecific depends upon two factors: 1) the coefficient of relatedness (r) of the parties, i.e., the proportion of genes shared by common descent, and 2) the ratio of recipient benefits to altruist costs. Thus, when r is high, altruistic behavior becomes highly probable if the recipient's benefit is high and the benefactor's cost is low. The result of Hamilton's work was a revised concept of fitness, "inclusive fitness." In contrast with the traditional concept of fitness, inclusive fitness refers to one's genetic contribution to future generations through both lineal and collateral relatives. Inasmuch as genes are shared by both kinds of kin, altruism toward siblings, cousins, and other collateral relatives could be expected to evolve when circumstances produce a favorable cost-benefit ratio.

Kin selection explains much of the cooperation and altruism observed in a wide variety of species, from ants to humans. However, it does not explain all cooperation and altruism, for cooperation and altruism may be found among nonrelatives as well as relatives. The foundation for this other type of cooperation and altruism is reciprocity (Williams 1966; Trivers 1971; Alexander 1974, 1979). When interactions between organisms are frequent, and cooperation or exchanges of altruistic behavior would be mutually beneficial, evolution should produce a capacity to make cost-benefit analyses as a basis for engaging in such behavior. This type of cooperation and altruism, labeled "reciprocal altruism" by Trivers (1971), has been found among and between many species of animals. It appears to be especially important among humans. Indeed, these genetically-based predispositions are almost certainly the foundation for much of the behavioral analyses found in the literature of public choice and game theory (e.g., Olson 1965; Margolis 1982; Axelrod 1984).*

Kin-selected cooperation and altruism entail immediate sacrifice for the benefactor but deferred genetic benefits across generations. Reciprocal altruism, by contrast, confers benefits during an organism's own lifetime, benefits that may indirectly result in greater reproductive success. Relatives may practice both kinds of cooperation and altruism among themselves, and for their ultimate genetic benefit. Among nonrelatives, only reciprocal altruism may be practiced for benefit; cooperation and altruism that do not produce lifetime benefits are practiced among nonrelatives only at genetic cost, and therefore only as evolutionary "mistakes."

A third foundation for social collaboration is exploitation - social behavior that benefits one party at the expense of another. For our purposes, these benefits must be of potential relevance to reproduction, thus tending to enhance the reproductive success of one party while diminishing that of the other. In some cases, the effect of exploitation on reproductive success may be direct and obvious. Thus, the cuckoo's practice of laying its eggs in the nests of other birds, often referred to as "social parasitism," is a clear-cut case of reproductive exploitation. This practice creates a social relationship (between cuckoo chick and surrogate parents) that clearly benefits one party (the mother cuckoo) while harming the other (the surrogate parents). Castration for the purpose of creating court eunuchs is another example. Barring benefits to kin that enhance their reproductive success enough to offset the loss of all personal reproduction, this practice tends to reduce the inclusive fitness of the eunuch while providing reproductively relevant benefits to the master.

In other cases of exploitation, effects may be indirect and more subtle. This is true of many cases of recognized parasitism, and is no doubt true of some relationships within animal societies founded primarily on nepotism and reciprocity. In human societies, for example, dishonest business practices transfer resources from one party to another, resources that might in the long run be converted into reproduction. Thus, those manipulated into buying a bottle of "snake oil" may not be harmed directly by the ineffective product they have purchased. However, if they are actually ill, purchase of this product may distract them from seeking treatment that might be genuinely effective, thereby increasing the probability of incapacitation or death. Or even if they are healthy and the product is harmless, they will have transferred reproductively relevant resources to another person without receiving a return benefit (assuming there are no reproductively relevant psychological benefits). This kind of social exchange, then, is exploitation.

Social relationships based solely upon exploitation are probably short-lived, relatively simple, or both. Thus, if the exploited party continues to reproduce within the context of the relationship, it will often evolve either to resist the exploitation or to garner some benefit from the relationship, thereby converting what began as exploitation into a relationship of mutual benefit. Even in instances in which exploitation is relatively enduring, counter selection should keep the relationship relatively simple. Thus, it seems unlikely that exploitation by itself could ever produce the complex web of relationships required to create animal societies. However, even if exploitation by itself is an inadequate foundation for social life, exploitation at some level should be found wherever social life is found.

Even if an instance of social life appeared solely on the basis of kin selection or reciprocity, some participants in the social relationships would almost inevitably evolve to exploit those relationships at some level. Exploitation will therefore normally evolve in tandem with the other two forms of social relationship. Thus, it is widely recognized that overt cheating will always be a problem in any system based upon reciprocity. The behavior of free riders is also exploitative, for free riders accept benefits from a relationship without contributing, thereby depriving other parties of the full benefits of the relationship.

These three evolutionary forces appear to account, singly or in combination, for most (if not all) cases of social life, from interspecific symbioses to ant colonies to ungulate herds to human societies. Nepotism and reciprocity both operate on a foundation of overlapping interests. In the case of kin selection, the overlapping interests are genetic and intergenerational. In the case of reciprocal altruism, the overlapping interests are nongenetic and intragenerational. In most cases, both forces will probably be operating, and they will probably also interact (Trivers 1971). Whenever either of these forces is at work, some level of exploitation should also emerge. For these reasons, all cases of complex social life are likely to involve a complicated mix of nepotism, reciprocity, and exploitation.

Kin selection and selection for reciprocal altruism produce long-term benefits for individuals. The cooperation and altruism that flow from such situations are therefore purely instrumental - they advance the interests of the component individuals. This means that all alliances, including whole societies, are instrumental entities - they exist to advance the interests, shared though they may be, of their component members.**
Since ethnic groups are alliances (or potential alliances), it is therefore likely that nepotism and reciprocity are the underlying sources of the cooperative behavior and identification processes responsible for ethnic identification. If we wish to understand ethnic conflict, then, we should investigate the mechanisms necessary for producing nepotism and reciprocity.

Recognizing Allies and Enemies
Humans bond to one another for the ultimate evolutionary reasons discussed above - there are advantages either across

generations of kin (nepotism) or within generations of kin or non-kin (reciprocity) that enhance reproductive success (on average). These ultimate advantages, however, can be realized only if there are proximate psychological mechanisms that trigger bonding based upon nepotism or reciprocity. Of course, mechanisms that identify threats and opportunities and assess costs and benefits must also be involved, but these mechanisms would have to work in conjunction with mechanisms that identify potential allies.

Nepotism appears to be the primary foundation for all societies of animals, from colonial invertebrates to eusocial insects to early humans (Wilson 1975; Alexander 1987). Thus, the most important source of cooperation and altruism in all of these systems appears to be kinship (even though reciprocity has also become important for some, especially humans). Kin-based cooperation and altruism, however, depend upon a capacity to recognize kin. If one is to bestow favors on kin, one must be able to discriminate between kin and non-kin, as well as between various degrees of kinship. In other words, there must be mechanisms of kin recognition.

Kin recognition does not require a cognitive awareness of kinship; it requires only that an animal discriminate behaviorally on the basis of some cue or cues that reflect levels of kinship. Hamilton recognized the importance of such mechanisms in his original path breaking article (1964), and proposed four possible mechanisms. The first of these mechanisms, direct genetic recognition ("recognition alleles"), is theoretically improbable. The other three mechanisms - association, phenotypic matching, and location - all work indirectly through observable cues that are correlated with kinship.

Since publication of Hamilton's article in 1964, the existence of these three indirect mechanisms of kin recognition has been confirmed. On the basis of one or more of these mechanisms, capacities for kin recognition have been empirically demonstrated for widely diverse species, including many species each of slime molds, sponges, insects, fishes, amphibians, birds, and mammals (Holmes and Sherman 1983; Sherman and Holmes 1985; Hepper 1986; Fletcher and Michener 1987; Waldman 1988; Alexander, 1990; Pfennig and Sherman 1995). These mechanisms, working together with other mechanisms, direct the social interactions of individuals with other individuals.

Theoretically, then, these mechanisms should influence the calculus underlying all social behavior. They will therefore be among the factors that determine, under particular circumstances, whether another animal will be considered a potential collaborator or a potential competitor. Under the right circumstances, operation of these mechanisms will prompt cooperation with those identified as kin; under the same circumstances, these mechanisms could prompt exploitation of those identified as non-kin. If ethnic identity is rooted in kinship or pseudo-kinship, as is often claimed, these mechanisms may be important generators of ethnic differentiation.

Association

For humans, as for many other species, typical arrangements for rearing offspring and for cooperative living in general bring kin into close association. Under such arrangements, those with whom one is most familiar are likely to be kin. On the basis of this correlation between familiarity and kinship, kin selection can act to produce kin-based cooperation and altruism by creating predispositions to "love," care for, cooperate with, and make sacrifices for close associates. The actual physical cues used for distinguishing familiar from unfamiliar conspecifics vary across species. Thus, many mammals rely especially (although not necessarily exclusively) on olfactory cues. Birds often rely on the unique characteristics of their comrades' vocalizations. And some species, including humans, depend heavily on visual cues. Regardless of which physical cues are used, however, kin recognition by association works through an empirically existing correlation between level of familiarity and level of kinship. Of course, since this is a probabilistic relationship, use of this mechanism is subject both to evolutionary "mistakes" and to manipulation.

Association is probably the most important kin recognition mechanism for humans. This seems likely, first, because hominids spent over 99% of their existence in small, relatively cohesive bands of kin. Second, daily living and rearing arrangements for most of human history would normally have made association the most reliable index of kinship. Third, humans are very good at recognizing and remembering the specific individuals with whom they associate. It seems likely, then, that the most important postpartum kin recognition mechanism for humans is association. Further support for this assumption is provided by the great importance of face recognition among humans. Humans are predisposed to pay special attention to the unique features of human faces. This is such an important function for humans that a specialized region of the brain is devoted to carrying it out (Geschwind 1979).

Association must have been a potent source of cohesion in band societies. With the temporary exception of those who married into the band from outside, the closest associates of everyone in the band were other band members. Initially, those who married into the group would be bonded through a lifetime of close association with those in another band - their native band. However, through cooperative living in the new group, and especially through rearing their own children within this group, even these outside members would have become bonded over time to that group.

Phenotypic Matching

Association is probably the most important kin recognition mechanism for humans, but phenotypic matching is probably another mechanism of considerable importance. It may also be a mechanism whose operation is an important key for understanding ethnic identification and conflict.

Phenotypic matching can serve as a mechanism of kin recognition because there is often a correlation between genotype and phenotype - those who are related are more similar phenotypically than those who are not, at least on average. Thus, for the purposes of discriminating between kin and non-kin, an animal can compare its own characteristics (or those of its close associates, who are probably kin) with the characteristics of other animals: the greater the similarity, the higher the probable level of kinship. The actual characteristics used for comparison vary across species. Appearance might be important for a visually oriented species, while vocalizations or smell might be important for other species.

This mechanism of kin recognition is found widely in nature. Thus, current evidence suggests that social insects such as honey bees and ants rely on it exclusively for distinguishing the fellow colony members from the members of other colonies (colony recognition) and for distinguishing varying degrees of relatedness within colonies (Winston 1987; Hölldobler and Wilson 1990). The matching takes place on the basis of pheromones, chemical substances produced in special glands and used for a variety of communication functions. In carpenter ant colonies, for example, this function is apparently coordinated by the queen, who distributes a pheromone that uniquely identifies members of the colony. By means of this chemical uniform, guards make decisions about whether to admit or repel an individual seeking admittance to the colony. These pheromonal cues are so important in governing the life of carpenter ant colonies that experimental manipulation can lead colony members to reject genetic sisters and accept not only unrelated individuals from other colonies, but even unrelated individuals of other species (Carlin and Hölldobler 1983).

Phenotypic matching is probably an important mechanism of kin recognition among humans, even if it is secondary relative to association (Alexander 1979; Essock-Vitale and McGuire 1980; van den Berghe 1981). While association provides useful cues for behavior when one is interacting with individuals of varying levels of familiarity, phenotypic matching would provide cues for behavior even when everyone was a total stranger. It would also serve as a useful supplement to association cues - among those whom I know equally well, those who are similar to me are likely to be more closely related than those who are dissimilar.

Since an animal's phenotype includes its behavior, phenotypic matching could be based on behavior as well as on physical characteristics. Among humans, this would even include behaviors that are heavily dependent upon experience, because those who share experience that affects future behavior - especially early in development - are often kin. Among humans, then, phenotype includes language, accent, idioms, customs, gestures, manners, dress and ornamentation, rituals, and other cultural characteristics. All of these phenotypic characteristics can serve to distinguish groups of people from one another. The various elements of this phenotypic uniform can set those allied together apart from others, and in nested sets based upon where interests overlap and diverge. All such phenotypic signals serve to distinguish those who are allied (originally because of kinship) from those who are external to the alliance and are either threats to the interests of those in the alliance or (from an evolutionary point of view) acceptable objects of exploitation.

Location

The third empirically confirmed mechanism of kin recognition depends upon a correlation between kinship and location. If individuals found in a particular location (e.g., a nest) are more likely to be kin than those in other locations, selection can produce behavioral discrimination based on location. Thus, prior to the time when their offspring fledge (when recognition by association can take over), birds use the location of their nests as a cue for kin recognition. Based upon this cue, they invest their energy - and perhaps even their lives - in caring for and defending the eggs or chicks who occupy that nest. Of course, it is this simple mechanism that the cuckoo exploits when she deposits her eggs in the nests of other birds.

Given that human hunter-and-gatherer bands were relatively mobile, it could be argued that location is an unlikely kin recognition mechanism for humans (Johnson 1986). However, we have several reasons for believing that humans retain some modest propensity to use location as a kin recognition device (see Johnson 1989, 64-65). Such a capacity would help explain what seems to be a tendency to hold the place of our rearing in special affection. It would also help explain why words, symbols, and images associated with this place are emotionally evocative. Thus, in addition to their association with kin, part of the power of such terms as "homeland," "hometown," and "land of our birth" may arise because location can act as a supplemental cue for altruistic dispositions.

Reciprocity

Assuming that conditions are right for cooperative behavior based upon reciprocity, and holding kin recognition cues constant, humans seem to rely heavily on experience as a guide for choosing who should be trusted as a cooperative partner. We obviously use our own experience as a guide (Axelrod and Hamilton 1981), but we also obviously attempt to make inferences from the experience of others (Alexander 1987). That is why reputation-building is such an important phenomenon. A reputation, which is built upon the experience of others with an individual's behavior, can be used to make inferences about future behavior. Of course, given the high level of shared interest with kin, we are likely to depend more heavily upon cues from kin than from others.

Alliance Expansion

These mechanisms of identifying allies and enemies must have worked reasonably well for most of human existence, during which humans lived in relatively small bands of mostly kin. More importantly for our purposes, however, these mechanisms - working together with other mechanisms - must have preadapted humans for building larger and more complex alliances. A trait is a preadaptation when it may be put, with or without refinement by natural selection, to uses other than those for which it originally evolved.

Beginning at least 12,000 years ago, after the earth had been widely populated with small hunter-and-gatherer bands, the size of the units in which many humans lived began to increase. In addition, more complex bonds were being forged between groups that lived apart, but in proximity. These developments were probably a response, within circumscribed environments, to population pressure, ecological change, and hostilities with other groups (Carneiro 1970). Despite numerous side-effects that had to be dealt with (e.g., through the growth of government - Johnson 1995), these new alliances allowed those allied together to accomplish new kinds of tasks in pursuit of overlapping interests. These broader alliances eventually created tribes, chiefdoms, states, and empires.

The easiest allies to make in this process, of course, would be those with whom one already had bonds under the operation of kin recognition mechanisms. This would certainly include other bands into which relatives had married. Prior association could therefore help generate stronger bonds between groups, but these bonds could be strengthened even further through phenotypic matching. Groups more recently fissioned from a common ancestor group would probably be more similar in language and a wide variety of cultural characteristics than groups that had been separated for longer. Other things being equal, those most phenotypically similar (keeping in mind that phenotype includes all behavior, and not just physical appearance) will be easiest to unite in an alliance.

If a permanent alliance with other groups is needed, the socialization process can be adjusted to manipulate both sets of powerful human kin recognition mechanisms. Thus, as in the case of patriotism, kin terms can be used fictively to help create emotional attachments to those toward whom one would not be naturally bonded by personal experience (Johnson 1986, 1987, 1997b; Johnson, Ratwik, and Sawyer 1987). And, drawing on the power of phenotypic matching, the attention of children may be drawn to the phenotypic similarities of these allies rather than their phenotypic differences. Likewise, when attention is drawn to dissimilarities between "us" and other groups - "them" - these others are identified as enemies (i.e., as threats to "us" and as evolutionarily acceptable objects of exploitation). We may view such manipulation of kin recognition mechanisms as a "social technology" (see Salter 2001).

Skipping forward for now, this brings us to use of the term "ethnic group," which is typically defined through some connection with kinship (e.g., van den Berghe 1981; Horowitz 1985; Connor 1994). From the perspective advanced here, ethnic groups are alliances or potential alliances that depend for their coherence on an orchestrated application of kin recognition mechanisms to individuals beyond the extended family. "Ethnic identity," therefore, should be the active or residual product of an alliance-building effort in which kin recognition mechanisms play an important role. This is not to suggest that other mechanisms are not important. Reciprocity-based mechanisms would also be important, as would mechanisms for recognizing collective goods, recognizing threats, and recognizing collective entities as units (see Johnson, 1997b). Nevertheless, what distinguishes ethnic groups from other kinds of human alliances is the relative importance of kin recognition mechanisms in the construction process.

If this position is correct, a number of phenomena widely observed about ethnic groups and ethnic identification are easily understandable. Thus, ethnic groups on this view are clearly both "primordial" and "instrumentalist" (as van den Berghe pointed out, 1981; cf. Eller and Coughlan 1993; McKay 1982). Also, if ethnic groups are alliances, and if alliances are the instruments of individuals pursuing their interests, we would also expect that ethnicity would be situational (Okamura 1981); that ethnic group boundaries would be flexible (Horowitz 1985); that operative phenotypic markers would be variable across ethnic groups and flexibly applied within ethnic groups according to need (Horowitz 1985); and that formerly antagonistic ethnic groups would often amalgamate over time to form new ethnic groups (Connor 1994). Of course, even if this perspective is correct, adequate understanding of these and other ethnic phenomena will require careful study of the processes through which kin recognition mechanisms - together with other mechanisms - are utilized.

Issues in Understanding Ethnic Conflict

I will turn now to a number of specific issues that relate to interpreting ethnic conflict from this perspective.

Phenotypic Matching - Pervasive Use, and Not Just Physical

It is important to emphasize two things about phenotypic matching as a human kin recognition device. First, it must again be emphasized that "phenotype" does not refer just to physical characteristics. "Phenotype" refers to all of an organism's observable physical and behavioral characteristics, including - in the case of humans - language, dialect, customs, diet, and so on. In other words, a human phenotype includes all of those "cultural" markers that are often used to distinguish ethnic groups.

Second, phenotypic matching almost certainly did not evolve to facilitate the formation of what we would today refer to as "ethnic groups." Its fundamental processes would have evolved originally simply to guide daily decision-making within and between the small kin-based groups in which humans have spent most of their existence. Once these mechanisms were in place, however, they would have helped guide behavior in situations that were relatively new, or even that had never before been encountered. Thus, it is probably not relevant that most humans, until recently, did not have contact with those of different races (cf. van den Berghe 1981, 240). If humans possess mechanisms designed by natural selection to be able to "detect" the relatively subtle differences that constitute what we refer to as "family resemblance," these mechanisms would surely have been activated when they began encountering those with very different physical (not to mention cultural) phenotypes. While these mechanisms certainly didn't evolve, then, to make humans racists, they are probably partly responsible for what many of us see as the dismaying pervasiveness and persistence of racism.

Multiple Mechanisms

If this perspective suggests new lines of research on the foundations of ethnic conflict and the socialization of ethnic identity, it should be emphasized that there are probably hundreds of mechanisms involved in producing and regulating ethnic conflict - and not just kin recognition mechanisms. Indeed, each of the kin recognition mechanisms referred to here in the singular could easily be composed of multiple component mechanisms. And there may also be mechanisms that govern how kin recognition mechanisms interact with each other (e.g., to regulate which takes precedence according to circumstance), how they interact with the mechanisms of reciprocity, and how they interact with experience (for a valuable discussion of the reasons for thinking of the human mind as a complex of many distinct mechanisms, see Tooby and Cosmides 1992).

Common Descent

Analysts of ethnic conflict frequently discuss a "myth of common descent" as binding together the members of an ethnic group, and this is occasionally the crucial defining characteristic. From an evolutionary perspective, the "myth of common descent" has at least an element of truth. Many (but certainly not all) of those who are included within the self-identified ethnic group are indeed descendants of people who have been allied together across multiple generations (through ties of kinship or reciprocity, and often both). This is no doubt one of the reasons that "myths of common descent" are so common - indeed, a defining characteristic according to Connor, 1994 - they reflect the fact that many of the people in question and many of their immediate forebears have been part of an alliance that extends across generations.

An ethnic group is, at best (and even when it is small), a highly diluted kin group. Nevertheless, its veiled core almost certainly consists of the descendants of a long-term, cross-generation alliance. New groups may have been added over the centuries - through peaceful alliance-making or conquest - but there is quite likely an unbroken series of links back through time to one or several original groups (even if not a single ancestral couple). These links are more than biological, for new members of the group in each generation have typically been socialized by their own kin, creating an unbroken chain of socialization across many generations.

The resulting similarities in a broad range of phenotypic (physical and cultural) characteristics, together with direct and indirect ties of association, can generate feelings of kinship among members of ethnic groups, especially when there is competition with those of differing phenotypic characteristics. There may be no identifiable common ancestor - indeed, the people in question may be an assimilated amalgam of different peoples, as the English are an amalgam of Celts, Angles, Saxons, Jutes, Danes, and Normans (Connor 1994, 214). There is, nevertheless, a genuine cross-generation continuity that reaches beyond the memories of even the oldest living members of the group, and probably far beyond, into what would be - from a folk perspective - the mists of the past.

Biological kinship may therefore be weak within large ethnic groups, but there are long, branching lines of intimate kin connections within these cross-generation alliances. These kinds of kin connections do not exist within many other kinds of alliances, which are formed primarily on the basis of relatively short-term mutual advantage. Thus, in contrast to members of ethnic groups, members of labor unions are (at least typically) neither born into the union nor socialized as members of the union by their own kin. Since humans should be predisposed to accept socialization efforts of kin over non-kin, these differences in group origin should result in important differences in group structure, cohesion, and behavior.

Let us now turn to the "myth" part of the "myth of common descent." Those who stress the kinship-related origin of nationalism or ethnicity (e.g., van den Berghe 1981; Horowitz 1985; Connor 1994) seem to have a much better appreciation of its roots than other analysts, and they also understand the tremendous emotive power of ethnicity. I greatly admire their work. However, I question whether it is a belief about common descent that provides the primary motive force behind ethnicity or nationalism. Why should an abstract claim about a common relationship to some long dead ancestor move people to acts of both enormous self-sacrifice and brutality? Millions of Christians from a variety of ethnic groups believe they are ancestrally related through Adam and Eve. This belief, however, does not seem to have bound these believers together in a nation; indeed, over the centuries, those who profess this belief have slaughtered one another by the millions.

So, is it really a "belief" that is relevant, or is it perceived phenotypic similarity and other kin recognition triggers (such as the use of kin terms in speech, songs, and poetry), and under specifiable conditions (especially threat), that creates the bonds of ethnicity? If the latter, a "belief" or "myth" of common descent is not the real foundation of ethnicity - the causal force - but rather only a manifestation of the underlying kinship identifying mechanisms.

It is not really the myths, then, that we need to study. We need to begin carefully investigating the day-to-day interactions and paraphernalia that build national consciousness. Thus, I wholeheartedly agree with Connor that those interested in understanding nationalism should carefully study nationalist poetry, speeches, pamphlets, and other such communications (Connor 1994, 75-76). They should also be studying the speech, gestures, and facial expressions of parents, other kin, and teachers as they socialize children to ethnic identity. Rather than searching for "beliefs" in those communications, however, they should be looking for the evocative use of kin terms and other triggers of kin recognition, interest identification, threat identification, etc.

Thus, there is an important difference between attributing causal importance to "myths of common descent" or "myths of fictive kinship" (Masters 1993) and "fictive use of kin terms" (which I have investigated in relation to patriotism - Johnson 1987, 1997b; Johnson, Ratwik, and Sawyer 1987). If we conceptualize fictive kinship as involving beliefs about kinship, it is presumably the idea of motherhood that creates the evocative influence of the term "motherland" in patriotic and nationalist speech and literature. As I conceptualize the process, however, there are no ideas or beliefs that travel between heads. Instead, what is at work in creating emotional significance for the term motherland is a multi-step process founded in kin recognition.

The word for "mother" is presumably an inherently neutral auditory stimulus in all human languages. However, this neutral auditory stimulus is generally applied to the person in one's experience who functions as one's mother - one's closest and most intimate caregiver early in life. One will be emotionally bonded to this most intimate associate through the kin recognition mechanism of association. Once this bonding has occurred, regular use of the word "mother" to represent this person should - through the simple process of classical conditioning - attach emotional significance to this word. The term itself therefore becomes capable of evoking powerful kinship-related emotions. This explains how kin terms such as mother, father, sister, and brother acquire their evocative significance. Thereafter, higher order conditioning on the kin term can transfer some of a kin term's emotional significance to the names of countries ("Mother Russia"), the names of ethnic groups (Tutsi brothers and sisters), and cultural symbols ("flag of your fathers"; see Johnson, 1997b).

To make the contrast clear, Roger Masters - in an article I admire - says that the French revolutionaries of 1789

> *openly proclaimed fictive kinship. The resulting spirit of community in what had been a highly diverse feudal monarchy with strong provincial and regional attachments generated the extraordinary dynamism of France after 1789. A hitherto untapped willingness to pay taxes and die for the State, repeated military successes both under the Republic and the First Empire, the forcible expulsion or killing of those who resisted (especially in the Terror), economic growth, development of centralized bureaucratic institutions - in short, the forging of a modern nation-state - coincided with the fiction that all members of the community... were "brothers."* (Masters 1993, 113-114; emphasis added)

As sympathetic as I am with the general import of this analysis, it seems an overstatement to attribute so much of the French Revolution to a myth of fictive kinship. On the other hand, the fictive use of kin terms probably did play a role, together with a great many other mechanisms. The difference between the two perspectives lies in whether one believes that a myth of kinship evoked all of this behavior, or whether - under the right circumstances - the application of kin terms toward non-kin, institutions, and systems is capable of associating some of the emotions felt toward kin with these non-kin, institutions, and systems. It is doubtful, after all, that the French revolutionaries *believed* they were kin.

If this theory is correct, one need not "believe" a myth of kinship to be influenced by the fictive use of kin terms. If an ethnic leader proclaims that all members of an ethnic group are brothers and sisters who must work and sacrifice together to establish a homeland, ***his or her listeners are unlikely to believe that several million people - most of whom they do not know - are their siblings. However, if they have been socialized properly, this use of kin terms may arouse emotions that could not be aroused merely on the basis of an appeal to shared interests.

Natural Selection and Proximate Mechanisms

Experimental research has shown that humans assigned randomly to artificially created groups will quickly display many of the characteristics we associate with the in-group–out-group mentality of ethnocentrism. Neither kinship nor familiarity is necessary. This could be interpreted as suggesting that these characteristics are not founded in the kinds of processes analyzed here (e.g., Ross 1991; Tullberg and Tullberg 1997). However, it must be remembered that natural selection is not a supernatural engineer that works from scratch and on short notice to create a product of perfect design for an organism's current environment. Natural selection works, over relatively long periods of time, on materials that are themselves the imperfect product of earlier selective compromises, and it designs on the basis of past experience, not current needs.

Thus, for the period in which human psychological mechanisms were designed, humans were seldom, if ever, thrown randomly into groups of people with whom they had had no previous contact. In the rare cases in which they might have been, they would have responded in terms of mechanisms "designed" for their customary social environment. Thus, it is not the least bit surprising that humans thrown into artificially created groups would quickly employ behavioral mechanisms normally used in other situations - they have no mechanisms designed by natural selection for the artificial situation.

Individual Level Selection versus Group Selection

There has been renewed interest recently in the possibility that human cooperation and altruism are at least partially a product of group selection - that is, differential extinction and reproduction of groups (e.g., Wilson and Sober, 1994). By contrast with kin selection and selection for reciprocal altruism, group selection could produce behavior that is individually disadvantageous even at the genetic level, so long as the behavior advanced the competitive interests of the groups whose members displayed these behaviors. This is appealing to some, because altruism generated by group selection could be thoroughly altruistic (not "tainted" by selfishness, even at the genetic level), and societies and other human alliances would not be merely instrumental. Of course, if group selection were implicated in the evolution of human altruism, our approach to understanding ethnicity and ethnic conflict would be correspondingly different.

Even though a contribution by group selection may not be ruled out, it seems doubtful that group selection has played a role of significance in the evolution of human cooperation and altruism. If the kind of human loyalty that is displayed toward countries and ethnic groups had been built by group selection (overwhelming the effects of individual counter selection), then loyalty to one's birth group should be genetically fixed. It makes little sense to suggest that group selection - which would build group loyalty even when it was individually disadvantageous - would endow individual humans with a capacity for strategically flexible loyalty. And yet that is exactly the kind of behavior that humans often display. This suggests that even if group selection sometimes reinforced the effects of individual selection, it has not been the primary force in the evolution of the human capacity for group loyalty.

Culture versus Biology

It is often said that ethnic identity is "socially constructed." Indeed it is, but it is not constructed from nothing. We may not be born with an ethnic identity, but we are born with - in fact conceived with - complex genetic blueprints that will, in relatively normal circumstances, help construct a mind sensitive to some environmental influences and insensitive to others. And, while we are not born a member of this or that ethnic group, we are born into nonrandom groups of compatriots (most often kin) who are predisposed to interact with us over the course of our development in ways that will instill in us a group identity.

To say, then, that ethnic identity is "socially constructed" is, by itself, to say very little - only that ethnic identity is not genetically fixed. To understand ethnic identity as a social construction, therefore, we must understand, among other things, the psychological mechanisms of those whose identities are being constructed, as well as the psychological mechanisms of those who are doing the constructing. Since those mechanisms are the long-term products of natural selection, we are likely to gain our best insights into these mechanisms by studying them from an evolutionary perspective. And, since contemporary human groups and societies seem to be design elaborations on the small hunting-and-gathering bands built by processes that included kin selection, we have good reason to think that some of the mechanisms harnessed for this purpose were built by kin selection.

The traditional dichotomous distinction between culture and biology (or human nature) is therefore artificial and misleading. **** Culture is not the antithesis of biology; culture is the expression of human biology under variable social, historical, and ecological conditions. For that reason, we are not abandoning culture when we employ an evolutionary perspective in our investigations; we are simply expanding the scope of our explanatory framework.

Conclusions

It has sometimes been claimed that evolutionary theories are inherently supportive of racism and ethnocentrism (not to mention sexism, imperialism, capitalism, and any other "ism" the anti-evolutionist opposes). This is, of course, absurd. An attempt to understand the evolution of HIV does not commit one to supporting AIDS. Only the most simple-minded ideologues take this position seriously. This is not to deny, however, that racists, imperialists, and others have sometimes attempted to draw support from evolutionary theory for their particular values; they have. But there is nothing unusual in this - the human mind seeks support for its preferences in any body of thought that may seem to lend authority to those preferences, whether that body of thought is science, religion, or the supposedly inspired insights of some social and political prophet.

More seriously, critics have often suggested that evolutionary theories commit one to accepting the world as it is (for example, that "racial and ethnic inequalities are to be expected and, for some at least, to be lived with" - Thompson 1989, 5). Again, there is no denying that some who prefer the world the way it is have sought support in evolutionary theory. However, revolutionary thinkers have also attempted to use evolutionary theory as support for their views (e.g., Marx, Engels, Bakunin, and Kropotkin). There is nothing in evolutionary theory that necessarily commits one to a defense of the status quo, just as there is nothing in evolutionary theory that would require bacteriologists and virologists to approve or passively accept tragedy and death from the diseases they study. On the contrary, these scientists are often passionately committed to fighting disease - and they believe, rightly, that understanding the evolutionary roots of these diseases (and of immune systems) will assist them in their fight.

We now know - seemingly without reasonable question - that human bodies and human brains are the long-term products of natural selection. We will therefore almost certainly formulate better theories about all forms of human behavior when we adopt an evolutionary perspective. The study of ethnic conflict should be no exception. If we can erect a new and better framework for studying this common and frequently violent phenomenon, then those with genuine substantive expertise in the area may see new patterns in their data, and they and their students may design new studies that will advance our understanding of ethnic conflict. We may even reasonably hope that a better understanding of the evolutionary roots of ethnic conflict may eventually help resolve some of those conflicts more peacefully.

Acknowledgments

This chapter was published originally in Patrick James and David Goetze (eds.), *Evolutionary Theory and Ethnic Conflict* (Westport, CT: Praeger 2001). It appears here with permission of the publisher (conveyed through Copyright Clearance Center, Inc.). Numerous passages were incorporated, with only minor revisions, from Johnson 1995, 1997a, 1997b, 1999.

Notes

* Authors sometimes distinguish among different kinds of cooperation/altruism based upon mutual benefit, depending upon such variables as whether an actual exchange takes place (simple mutualism may not involve an exchange), how soon reciprocation takes place, whether reciprocation is made by the original recipient or by others who are involved in a complex system of indirect reciprocity, etc. (e.g., Corning 1983; Alexander 1987). These distinctions are important for some purposes, but for the purposes of this article, all such instances will be considered special cases of the broad phenomenon of cooperation and altruism that is not dependent upon cross-generation genetic benefits. For convenience, I refer to all such cases as instances of reciprocal altruism.

** This is not to say that the benefits of an alliance are equally distributed. Some members may benefit more than others. And some may be exploited but have no reasonable alternative - they must accept the exploitation because the alternatives are worse.

*** Since the word "home" will be linked by classical conditioning to the people in one's home - typically one's kin - the term "homeland" itself functions as an indirect kin term.

**** Or as Goetze and James have put it: "Cultural processes do not operate autonomously from evolutionary processes" (2001, 15).

References

Alexander, Richard D. 1974. "The Evolution of Social Behavior." *Annual Review of Ecology and Systematics* 5:325-83.

Alexander, Richard D. 1979. *Darwinism and Human Affairs.* Seattle, WA: University of Washington Press.

Alexander, Richard D. 1987. *The Biology of Moral Systems.* New York: Aldine de Gruyter.

Alexander, Richard D. 1990. "Epigenetic Rules and Darwinian Algorithms: The Adaptive Study of Learning and Development." *Ethology and Sociobiology* 11:241-303.

Axelrod, Robert. 1984. *The Evolution of Cooperation.* New York: Basic Books.

Axelrod, Robert and William D. Hamilton. 1981. "The Evolution of Cooperation." *Science* 211:1390-96.

Carlin, Norman F. and Bert Hölldobler. 1983. "Nest Mate and

Kin Recognition in Interspecific Mixed Colonies of Ants." *Science* 222:1027-29.

Carneiro, Robert L. 1970. "A Theory of the Origin of the State." *Science* 169:733-38.

Connor, Walker. 1994. *Ethnonationalism: The Quest for Understanding.* Princeton, NJ: Princeton University Press.

Corning, Peter A. 1983. *The Synergism Hypothesis: A Theory of Progressive Evolution.* New York: McGraw-Hill.

Dawkins, Richard. 1976. *The Selfish Gene.* New York: Oxford University Press.

Dawkins, Richard. 1982. *The Extended Phenotype: The Gene as the Unit of Selection.* Oxford: Oxford University Press.

Eller, Jack David and Reed M. Coughlan. 1993. "The Poverty of Primordialism: The Demystification of Ethnic Attachments." *Ethnic and Racial Studies* 16:183-202.

Essock-Vitale, Susan M. and Michael T. McGuire. 1980. "Predictions Derived from the Theories of Kin Selection and Reciprocation Assessed by Anthropological Data." *Ethology and Sociobiology* 1:233-44.

Fletcher, David J.C. and Charles D. Michener, eds. 1987. *Kin Recognition in Animals.* New York: John Wiley.

Fox, Robin. 1994. "Nationalism: Hymns Ancient and Modern." *The National Interest* 35:51-57.

Geschwind, Norman. 1979. "Specializations of the Human Brain." *Scientific American* 24(3): 180-99.

Goetze, David and Patrick James. 2001. "What Can Evolutionary Theory Say About Ethnic Phenomena?" *In Evolutionary Theory and Ethnic Conflict*, eds. Patrick James and David Goetze. Westport, CT: Praeger.

Hamilton, William D. 1964. "The Genetical Evolution of Social Behavior I and II." *Journal of Theoretical Biology* 7:1-52.

Hepper, Peter G. 1986. "Kin Recognition: Functions and Mechanisms, A Review." *Biological Reviews of the Cambridge Philosophical Society* 61:63-93.

Hölldobler, Bert and Edward O. Wilson. 1990. *The Ants.* Cambridge, MA: Harvard University Press.

Holmes, Warren G. and Paul W. Sherman. 1983. "Kin Recognition in Animals." *American Scientist* 71:46-55.

Horowitz, Donald. 1985. *Ethnic Groups in Conflict.* Berkeley, CA: University of California Press.

Johnson, Gary R. 1986. "Kin Selection, Socialization, and Patriotism: An Integrating Theory" [with commentaries and response]. *Politics and the Life Sciences* 4:127-54.

Johnson, Gary R. 1987. "In the Name of the Fatherland: An Analysis of Kin Term Usage in Patriotic Speech and Literature." *International Political Science Review* 8:165-74.

Johnson, Gary R. 1989. "The Role of Kin Recognition Mechanisms in Patriotic Socialization: Further Reflections." *Politics and the Life Sciences* 8:62-69.

Johnson, Gary R. 1995. "The Evolutionary Origins of Government and Politics." In Human Nature and Politics, eds. Albert Somit and Joseph Losco. Greenwich, CT: JAI Press.

Johnson, Gary R. 1997a. "The Architecture of Ethnic Identity." *Politics and the Life Sciences* 16:257-262.

Johnson, Gary R. 1997b. "The Evolutionary Roots of Patriotism." In *Patriotism in the Lives of Individuals and Nations,* eds. Daniel Bar-Tal and Ervin Staub. Chicago: Nelson-Hall.

Johnson, Gary R., Susan H. Ratwik, and Timothy J. Sawyer. 1987. "The Evocative Significance of Kin Terms in Patriotic Speech." In *The Sociobiology of Ethnocentrism: Evolutionary Dimensions of Xenophobia, Discrimination, Racism and Nationalism,* eds. Vernon Reynolds, Vincent Falger, and Ian Vine. London: Croom Helm.

Margolis, Howard. 1982. *Selfishness, Altruism, and Rationality: A Theory of Social Choice.* Cambridge: Cambridge University Press.

Masters, Roger D. 1993. "On the Evolution of Political Communities: The Paradox of Eastern and Western Europe in the 1990's." In *Human Nature and the New Europe,* ed. Michael T. McGuire. Boulder, CO: Westview.

Maynard Smith, John. 1964. "Group Selection and Kin Selection." *Nature* 201:1145-47.

Maynard Smith, John. 1976. "Group Selection." *Quarterly Review of Biology* 51:277-83.

McKay, James. 1982. "An Exploratory Synthesis of Primordial and Mobilizationist Approaches to Ethnic Phenomena." *Ethnic and Racial Studies* 5:395-420.

Okamura, Jonathan Y. 1981. "Situational Ethnicity." *Ethnic and Racial Studies* 4:452-65.

Olson, Mancur. 1965. *The Logic of Collective Action: Public Goods and the Theory of Groups.* Cambridge, MA: Harvard University Press.

Pfennig, David W. and Paul W. Sherman. 1995. "Kin Recognition." *Scientific American* 272:98-103.

Reynolds, Vernon, Vincent Falger, and Ian Vine, eds. 1987. *The Sociobiology of Ethnocentrism: Evolutionary Dimensions of Xenophobia, Discrimination, Racism and Nationalism.* London: Croom Helm.

Ross, Marc Howard. 1981. "When Does Ethnic Antagonism Displace Class Conflict? A Sociobiological Hypothesis in Urban Africa." *Comparative Urban Research* 8:5-28.

Ross, Marc Howard. 1991. "The Role of Evolution in Ethnocentric Conflict and Its Management." *Journal of Social Issues* 47:167-85.

Salter, Frank. 2001. "A Defense and an Extension of Pierre van den Berghe's Theory of Ethnic Nepotism." In *Evolutionary Theory and Ethnic Conflict,* eds. Patrick James and David Goetze. Westport, CT: Praeger.

Shaw, R. Paul and Yuwa Wong. 1989. *Genetic Seeds of Warfare: Evolution, Nationalism, and Patriotism.* Boston: Unwin Hyman.

Sherman, Paul W. and Warren G. Holmes. 1985. "Kin Recognition: Issues and Evidence." In *Experimental Behavioral Ecology and Sociobiology,* eds. Bert Hölldobler and Martin Lindauer. Sunderland, MA: Sinauer Associates.

Thompson, Richard H. 1989. *Theories of Ethnicity: A Critical Appraisal.* New York: Greenwood Press.

Tooby, John and Leda Cosmides. 1992. "The Psychological Foundations of Culture." In *The Adapted Mind,* eds. Jerome H.

Barkow, Leda Cosmides and John Tooby . New York: Oxford University Press.

Trivers, Robert L. 1971. "The Evolution of Reciprocal Altruism." *Quarterly Review of Biology* 46:35-57.

Trivers, Robert L. 1974. "Parent-Offspring Conflict." American Zoologist 14:249-64.

Tullberg, Jan and Birgitta S. Tullberg. 1997. "Separation or Unity? A Model for Solving Ethnic Conflicts." *Politics and the Life Sciences* 16:237-248.

van den Berghe, Pierre L. 1981. *The Ethnic Phenomenon.* New York: Elsevier.

Waldman, Bruce. 1988. "The Ecology of Kin Recognition." *Annual Review of Ecology and Systematics* 19:543-71.

Warnecke, A. Michael, Roger D. Masters, and Guido Kempter. 1992. "The Roots of Nationalism: Nonverbal Behavior and Xenophobia." *Ethology and Sociobiology* 13:267-82.

Williams, George C. 1966. *Adaptation and Natural Selection: A Critique of Some Current Evolutionary Thought.* Princeton, NJ: Princeton University Press.

Wilson, D.S. and E. Sober (1994). "Reintroducing Group Selection to the Human Behavioral Sciences" [with commentaries and response]. *Behavioral and Brain Sciences* 17:585-654.

Wilson, Edward O. 1975. *Sociobiology: The New Synthesis.* Cambridge, MA: The Belknap Press of Harvard University Press.

Winston, Mark L. 1987. T*he Biology of the Honey Bee.* Cambridge, MA: Harvard University Press.

BIOLOGICAL PERSPECTIVES ON INTER-GROUP CONFLICT
Robert Sapolsky

Us-Them Dichotomy

The most unique thing is how (the) ancient neurobiology is harnessed in the service of the most astonishingly abstract dichotomies, ones that can be displaced over vast time and space.

Viewed from the perspective of mammalian social behavior, humans present a seeming paradox. We are, by far, the most violent species on the planet. We kill our conspecifics in numbers that dwarf the occasional murderousness of other primates. We can do so with a detachment that allows killing individuals whose faces we never even see, and with tools that include atomic bombs, automatic weapons and shower heads that deliver poison gas. Yet, amid such violence, we are simultaneously the most altruistic and cooperative species in existence. We build societies run on consensual laws, enter burning buildings to save strangers, and support charities that aid people we have never met.

Making sense of these two extremes requires recognizing our permeating human tendency to divide the world into in-groups and out-groups, and with the most violent of our behaviors aimed at Thems, and the most pro-social reserved for those who qualify as Us.

In this review, I consider the biology of human Us/Them dichotomizing, a subject that must encompass everything from the previous second's neuronal activity to the previous million years' evolutionary forces. A major theme emerges from such biology, namely that when it comes to the neurobiology and endocrinology of our social behavior, humans are constructed from the same general blueprint as other mammals; however, we then utilize that biology in novel manners. For example, humans can fall in love in ways dependent on the neurohormones vasopressin and oxytocin, much as when prairie voles pair-bond for life. However, we can love someone we have only met online, someone whose pheromones we have never smelled. Similarly, humans activate the brain's anterior cingulate cortex when feeling someone else's pain, much as in other species that show the rudiments of empathy. However, we can do so in response to the travails of a movie character, mere pixels on a screen. As will be seen, much of what accounts for both the most destructive and the most hopeful features of inter-group behavior reflects this theme of humans utilizing conventional biology in unconventional ways.

The extreme nature of Us/Them dichotomizing in humans and other species

A romanticized view of the natural world generated a supposed human uniqueness – we are the only species that kills its own kind. Decades of ethology research has undone this myth. An example is primates such as langur monkeys that carry out competitive infanticide, where males kill the likely offspring of other males (Hausfater & Hrdy, 1984). Or more commonly, males kill each other in the context of male-male competition for social dominance and reproductive access to females; among the baboons that I have studied, a leading cause of death of male baboons is male baboons (Sapolsky, 2001). Chimpanzee males battle each other with what as aptly been termed "political" skills and "Machiavellian" intelligence (de Waal, 1983; Maestripieri, 2007). And implicit in these descriptions is another commonality between violence in humans and most other animals, namely that it is mainly carried out by males.

Moreover, we are not the only species with organized, fatal violence between groups. The adult males in a chimpanzee group often carry out what are appropriately termed "border patrols," and if they encounter a male from a neighboring group, he will be attacked in a frenzy of coordinated violence. Remarkably, such inter-group aggression can extend to the point where all of the males of one group are eradicated, and with the triumphant males then expanding their territory (Peterson & Wrangham, 1997). Thus, we are not the only species displaying the essence of genocide, where individuals are killed not for who they are, but merely because of their group membership.

We and some other primates do not only share an often-bloody antipathy towards out-group members. We also share the capacity for Thems to elicit negative, implicit associations. This is demonstrated in humans with the Implicit Association Test (IAT). A subject watches a computer screen, having to rapidly make decisions – if shown the face of an in-group member, they must push one button; if the face of an out-group member, push a different button. Interspersed with this is a second task, where one of the two buttons is pressed if the screen display a word with a positive connotation (e.g., "honest" or "kind"), and the other button for a negative term ("malicious" or "harsh"). Once baseline response rates are determined, the two tasks are combined, where one button is pushed when seeing the face of one group or one type of term, the other button for the opposite.

Something fascinating emerges: people make faster, more accurate determinations when the task is to yoke positive words with in-group faces and negative terms with out-group than during the reverse (when in-group is yoked with negative and out-group with positive). Linking, say, the face of an in-group member with the word "generous" is simple; linking it with a Them causes a fraction of a second pause, because of the cognitive dissonance of the pairing. Importantly, implicit biases like these, as shown with the IAT, predict people's negative automatic and unintended behaviors towards out-group members (Nosek, Hawkins, & Frazier, 2011).

Remarkably, other primates also have implicit, automatic negative associations with Thems, as shown in a clever study that adapted the IAT for another species (Mahajan et al., 2011). Monkeys were trained to carry out a similar task: press one button for a picture of a member of their group, press the other for a strange monkey; press one button for a picture of something positive, the other for something negative. And when the two categories were combined, there was the same processing delay – it was easier and faster to associate group members with, say, fruit and strangers with spiders than the reverse.

Thus, humans are not unique in their capacity for murderous inter-group conflict, or for the subtlety of having automatic, negative associations with Thems. Naturally, there are vastly interesting differences between us and other species. To begin, other animals kill over territory or overt reproductive competition. However, we are unique in killing about ideas, beliefs and values – over the nature of deities, the relative merits of capitalism versus communism, or whether a flag should be honored or desecrated. We are unique in such abstractions.

We are also unique in the speed with which arbitrary groupings become meaningful. In a "minimum group" paradigm, a group is divided into two with coin tosses. And although participants fully understand the random nature of the assignments, preferential in-group cooperation and biases soon emerge (Tajfel, 1970, 1982). No equivalent in other species has been demonstrated.

The fact that we humans can kill over abstractions emphasizes our use of symbols. Observe a naked, unadorned human and you will have no idea of their beliefs. However, if they are dressed in jeans, cowboy boots and hat, they probably believe it is permissible to kill and eat cows, whereas if they are wearing a sari, they probably worship and protect them. Similarly, you can make some informed guesses about someone's economic power if their face is adorned with marks of scarification rituals and lip plugs versus false eyelashes and the tell-tale tautness of a face lift. Or just consider how symbolic variations in the appearance of a man's beard and how he covers his head predicts whether he thinks it is Muslims or Jews who should occupy Jerusalem. Numerous species, including humans, are subject to Pavlovian conditioning, where an arbitrary unconditioned stimulus (e.g., a distinctive bell or buzzer, a style of clothing or music) becomes yoked to a meaningful one (a shock, a reward, the knowledge that you are among friends versus enemies). We are unique, however, in the power with which we imbue arbitrary, symbolic markers of group membership. And so we have the human horror of urban gang-members killing someone because they are wearing clothing that is the color of another gang, or soldiers from opposing sides fighting over possessions of a regimental flag.

Thus, like many other species, we kill out-group members in organized, genocidal ways; unlike any other, we classify in- versus out-group membership based on cognitively sophisticated abstractions. However, our typical inability to accept the arbitrariness of our groupings shows the limits of our cognitive sophistication; this would be a more peaceful planet if we truly understood that the sheer randomness of where and to whom we were born determined which particular cause we would fervently kill or die for. We are the only species smart enough to understand this, but rarely do.

The nature of in-group interactions in humans and other species

It is in our interactions with fellow group members where humans most often display the best of our behaviors. Such pro-sociality shows striking continuity between us and other animals, particularly in the domains of cooperation, altruism and empathy.

There is a deep vein of cooperative and altruistic behavior in social species, reflecting shared evolutionary roots. Natural selection theory views social behavior as having evolved from three building blocks:

a) Individual Selection, the notion that organisms do not behave for "the good of the species" but, rather, to maximize their own individual fitness, leaving as many copies of their genes as possible in future generations.

b) Kin Selection, built on the fact that we share genes with relatives and share a greater percentage of them with closer relatives; as a result, sometimes, an animal can optimize the number of copies of its genes it leaves in future generations by aiding relatives to enhance their reproductive success. This explains when cooperative behavior in social species is heavily built along lines of kinship (starting with the obvious fact that maternal care is typically invested in your offspring, with whom you share half your genes, rather than in a stranger's offspring). Kin Selection is aptly summed with the quip, "I would gladly lay down my life to save the lives of two brothers [each sharing half your genes if full siblings] or eight cousins [each sharing one eighth of your genes if first cousins]."

c) Reciprocal Altruism, built around the notion that it can be evolutionarily advantageous to cooperate with unrelated strangers, so long as they reciprocate. Such contingent cooperation increases in likelihood in species where individuals live in stable social groups. As a key wrinkle in this picture, there is also selection for cheating on a relationship (i.e., deriving benefits without reciprocating) whenever possible, and for detecting and punishing cheaters; social species have evolved the means to navigate these issues with patterns of behavior best modeled by surprisingly sophisticated game theory.

Given these foundations, it is not surprising that cooperative behavior occurs most readily within, rather than between groups in social species. The sin qua non is in most social insects with sterile worker castes serving their sister queen, thanks to a unique genetics that greatly facilitates kin selection. But the same holds closer to home, among social mammals. For example, among African hunting dogs and chimpanzees, males spend their lives in the same group (with females migrating outward around puberty), producing high degrees of relatedness among males; in both species, such individuals are characterized by cooperative hunts and food-sharing (Creel & Marusha, 2002; Goodall, 2010). Among savanna baboons, it is females who remain in the troop their entire lives, where altruistic behavior (e.g., grooming someone, defending them in a fight, carrying their infant) is most common along lines of relatedness. Furthermore, cooperation among non-relatives shows the power of reciprocal altruism; for example, the best predictor of which non-relative a female baboon grooms is who has groomed her in the past (Altmann, 2001). Crucially then, the twin selective forces of kin selection and reciprocal altruism explain why cooperation is more common within rather than between groups.

Related to such contingent altruistic behavior, a growing literature shows the rudiments of empathy in other species. In some other primate and rodent species, victims of aggression will be preferentially groomed; observing another individual in pain lowers the observer's own pain threshold; individuals will exert effort and forgo reward to lessen another individual's distress (Rice & Gainer, 1962; Langford et al., 2006; Bartal,

Decety, & Mason, 2011; de Waal & Preston, 2017). Furthermore, the continuity between pro-social human empathy and such behavior in other species has similar biological roots, involving oxytocin and vasopressin, and the anterior cingulate cortex. Importantly, empathy-like behavior in other species is rife with in-group preference – another individual's pain lowers a rodent's own pain threshold only if the two know each other; victims of aggression or in distress in general will evoke pro-social behavior only if they are a group member, a mate, or a relative. It is not only humans where a stranger's pain does not count for much.

Collectively, these studies show that we are not the only species that is preferentially pro-social, cooperative and empathic with in-group members. This is where the differences emerge. What constitutes an in-group member for another primate? Typically, someone who has long slept in the same grove of trees each night that you do, foraging alongside you each day. In contrast, for humans, an in-group member can also be someone who shares nebulous cultural constructs like theology, ideology, or nationalism. And these are not mere proxies for living in proximity to and being familiar with someone; for example, in economic games, people make more generous offers if they believe the other player is a co-religionist, even if they have not met (Tajfel, 1970).

Where humans diverge most dramatically from other animals with respect to in-group behavior concerns kin selection and relatedness. How do rodents know who is related to them and to what extent? It is instinctual, where animals have olfactory pheromonal signatures that reflect their genetic makeup; the closer someone's pheromones are to your own, the closer the relative. Humans, in contrast, have only weak instinctual mechanisms for recognizing relatives (Jacob, McClintock, Zelano, & Ober, 2002). For the most part we have to think about it. We have to learn who married whom, who someone's children are. Most importantly, humans can feel related to someone else and act accordingly, completely independently of whether they are in fact genetically related. This is the phenomenon of "pseudo-kinship." Depending on your culture, a sister-in-law can be treated the same as a sister. An unrelated individual who you spent large amounts of intimate time with in your first years of life may be someone you love dearly, but who will never feel like a potential mate because it would seem incestuous (Shepher, 1971). Someone born on the other side of the planet can be adopted and raised as someone's beloved child. Two people in the same revolutionary vanguard might greet each other as siblings, addressing each other in their language's informal personal pronouns reserved for family. People may treat each other pro-socially as pseudo-kin if they wear the same religious garb, including the pseudo-religious garb of a cap whose logo indicates that they root for the same sports team. And throughout history, military training has involved rituals of pseudo-kinship to the point of making an unrelated fighting unit feel like a "band of brothers" willing to sacrifice their lives for each other; as a striking example, in World War II, a German-American soldier fighting in Europe might have shot a German who, unbeknownst to him, was a distant cousin, while defending the life of his buddy, a Mexican-American soldier with whom he went through basic training. In other words, while a mouse knows who it is related to by instinct, we can be manipulated into feeling more related to someone than we actually are.

As such, humans are completely unique in what can constitute an in-group member. Moreover, such decisions can be highly culture-specific. For example, in one study of employees in a multinational bank, American employees were most likely to do a favor for someone who had previously done the same for them, Spanish employees were most likely for friends and acquaintances, while Chinese employees were most likely for someone high-ranking (Morris, Podolny, & Ariel, 2000).

More realms of human uniqueness follow. Like many other species, we find in-group members to be more trustworthy (insofar as we are willing to act altruistically with an expectation of reciprocity) and we feel their pains more than those of strangers. But we are unique in believing that our in-group compatriots are more loving parents or write better folk music; we are unique in feeling a sense of obligation over shared sacred values (about, for example, a particular flag). We are the only species that explains away the transgressions of an in-group member situationally ("he was under a lot of stress at the time") while condemning the transgression of an out-group member by attributing constitutional traits to them ("he's rotten, always has been, always will be").

Finally, as a point whose significance will grow even larger in this review, humans uniquely belong to multiple groups at the same time. Crucially, which in-group membership seems most important to us at any particular time can shift dramatically.

The nature of inter-group interactions in humans and other species

It is in the realm of interactions between Us and Them that humans show both some of their most striking continuities and discontinuities with other species.

Starting with the former, the neurobiological underpinnings of our responses to out-group members is highly conserved across the animal kingdom. Central to this is the amygdala, a key structure in the limbic system that is central to fear, anxiety and aggression. Across a wide range of experimental species and humans as well, the amygdala activates in response to novel, fear-evoking stimuli; electrical stimulation of the amygdala causes unprovoked aggression; surgical or disease-related destruction of the amygdala blocks fear responses and aggressive behavior (LeDoux,1998; Zald, 2003; Feinstein, Adolphs, Damasio & Tranel, 2011). Its function is modulated by hormones in revealing ways. As one example, stress and the subsequent secretion of glucocorticoid stress hormones augments amygdaloid excitability, helping to explain poor aggressive impulse control that is common in highly stressful circumstances (Rodrigues, LeDoux, & Sapolsky, 2009). Moreover, the amygdala is extremely sensitive to the effects of testosterone, with high concentrations of receptors for the hormone; testosterone lowers the threshold for excitability of neurons in the amygdala, biasing organisms towards perceiving social stimuli as threatening (Kendrick & Drewett, 1979; Hermans, Ramsey, & von Honk, 2008).

The role of the amygdala in responding to out-group members has provided one of the most unsettling observations in social neuroscience. This well-replicated finding involves human subjects undergoing functional brain imaging while being shown faces of people for a fraction of a second each. Remarkably, in the average subject, seeing the face of a human of a different race causes activation of the amygdala within a tenth of a second. In other words, before there is even conscious awareness of the face being observed, the amygdala reacts to someone considered to be an out-group member (Hart et al., 2000; Golby, Gabrieli, Chiaio, & Eberhardt, 2001). An equally distressing finding concerns the fusiform cortex, a specialized primate brain region that is key to recognizing individual faces; in the average subject, the face of someone of another race causes less activation than a same-race face – brains individuate and differentiate faces of out-group members less than of in-group members (to my knowledge, an equivalent study has not been done with non-human primates) (Kubota, Banaji, & Phelps, 2012). Finally, the use of the word "average" twice in this paragraph indicates that not all humans respond this way; as will be discussed below, the exceptions are revealing.

The role of emotion in human inter-group conflict reflects another commonality with other species. There is little reason to believe that the males in a chimpanzee band try to kill strange males living to the west as well as those living to the east, but for different reasons. Instead, in-group/out-group hostility in other species reflects undifferentiated emotion. There is much to suggest that the same typically holds in humans. Consider an individual with a bias against one out-group because of their sexual practices, against another because of their economic beliefs, and another because of an ancient historical event. Such individuals rarely have arrived at those prejudices out of separate and distinctive cognitive paths; instead, studies suggest that the commonality is the person's underlying personality, with a visceral aversion to novelty and ambiguity, and a strong preference for hierarchy (Cunningham, Nezlek, & Banaji, 2004). Arguing further against the primacy of cognition in frequent cases of human inter-group conflict, there are long-standing out-group hostilities where people do not even know the reason for the hostility (e.g., consider the Cagots, a group in France that has been discriminated against since the 11th century, for no clear historical reason). In other words, as in other species, our out-group hostilities are typically rooted in emotion, rather than cognition. This dovetails with a theme in social neuroscience, namely that people typically feel their way, rather than think their way to moral decisions; in such cases, the rationale then offered to explain the decision is actually post-hoc rationalization generated to be consonant with intuitive emotional decisions (Haidt, 2001, 2012). As one fascinating manifestation of this, when subjects contemplate scenarios of possible moral transgressions, activation in the limbic system can both predict their assessment and precede activation in the cortex (Sanfey, Rilling, Aronson, Nystrom, & Cohen, 2003; Haruno & Frith, 2010).

Continuing this emphasis on the centrality of emotions, human out-group violence is subject to emotional contagion, as in other species. Among male baboons, an individual attacking someone lower-ranking often prompts another male to join in.

Among male chimpanzees, a border patrol begins with one chimp performing agitated, aggressive displays, who is then joined by the rest. The dangers of social contagion in group violence among humans is well known, prompting Reinhold Niebuhr (1941) to write, "The group is more arrogant, hypocritical, self-centered and more ruthless in the pursuit of its ends than the individual."

Thus, humans, along with other social animals, share the neurobiological underpinnings of out-group hostility, the primacy of emotions in driving such states, and the danger of the group. This is where the differences become most important, perhaps best summarized by the fact that while emotional contagion in chimpanzees involves males in close proximity carrying out frenzied displays together before attempting to kill a stranger, humans can do so by seeing a propagandistic poster, or reading a tweet dripping with poisonous intent. It is here where human social abstraction dominates. As I will now review, this takes at least three forms: a) not all out-groups are the same; b) we belong to multiple in-groups simultaneously, each with its own distinctive out-group; c) which in-/out-group difference is most important to us can shift.

The taxonomy of human out-groups

The negative behaviors expressed towards out-group members in other species sits in an amygdaloid nexus of fear and aggression. In contrast, humans categorize different out-groups differently, in both cognitive and emotional dimensions.

The "stereotype content" model of Susan Fiske of Princeton University shows that we categorize out-groups along two separate axes (Fiske, Cuddy, Glick, & Xu, 2002; Harris & Fiske 2006, 2007). The first concerns how we perceive out-groups on a scale of their intent – are they benevolent, malevolent or somewhere in between? The second concerns how effective we think they are at carrying out their intent – are they competent agents, ineffectual and innocuous, or in between? From these two independent axes come very different responses to different out-groups.

To begin by stating the obvious, those who are categorized as high in both benevolent "warmth" and in efficacious "competence" are de facto Us, reflecting the biases that we carry about in-group members as kind and capable.

At the other extreme are groups viewed as low in both warmth and competence. American subject show these associations for groups such as drug addicts and the homeless. Fiske has shown that such groups do not evoke hostility so much as disgust and a desire to avoid. Fascinatingly, pictures of such individuals do not typically activate the amygdala. Instead, there is activation of the insular cortex, a brain region which is responsive in mammals by gustatory disgust, by the taste or smell of rancid food; once activated, it triggers reflexes related to spitting the food out, gagging, and vomiting. This is the reason why people and actions that are morally disgusting can make us feel sick to our stomachs, queasy, and leave us with a bad taste in our mouths. In other words, the same neurons that process a disgusting, spoiled piece of food respond to a repellant out-group member in the low warmth/low competence category.

One of the adjacent corners of Fiske's two-axis model is filled with out-group members who are viewed as high in warmth but low in competence. This would be the loved relative sunk into dementia or the developmentally impaired individual, and the emotion most readily prompted by them is pity. Commensurate with that, such individuals do not activate the amygdala. Instead, there is typically activation of the anterior cingulate cortex which, as noted, is implicated in empathy.

The final category of out-group members in this matrix concerns individuals who are viewed as low in warmth but high in competence. These are minority groups who are viewed as cold, clannish, but capable and malevolent – for example, the unassimilated out-group that is particularly economically successful. History is replete with such examples, such as the traditional view of Jews in Europe, of Indo-Pakistanis in East Africa, or ethnic Chinese in Malaysia. It is in this realm that out-groups evoke the ugliest human emotions – hatred and envy, fueled by a frenzied amygdala. It is here that we have the roots of pogroms and genocides.

When violence is turned on a hated, envied low-warmth/high-competence outgroup, something frequently occurs. When Idi Amin expelled Ugandan citizens of Indo-Pakistani descent, he invited other Ugandans to rob, beat and rape them. When the firebrands of the Chinese Cultural Revolution turned on the intellectual elite, the latter were dragged through the streets in dunce caps. When Hitler's regime began the genocide of the Jews, individual victims were often forced by mobs to scrub the sidewalk with toothbrushes. There is an appalling human tendency, when turning violently upon envied low-warmth/high-competence minorities to first degrade them into seeming low competence – powerless, naked and humiliated.

The multiplicity of in-group memberships
When it comes to inter-group conflict, a key distinction between humans and other animals is our unique capacity to belong to, and identify with a variety of in-groups, based on race, age, gender, ethnicity, religious affiliation, political views, and so on. Crucially, which of our particular in-groups seems most important can shift. A classic example of this was a 1999 study built around two stereotypes, namely that people of Asian descent are atypically good at math, while women are typically worse at math than are men. In the experiment, Asian-American women took a math test; just before it began, half were prompted to identify with their gender, half with their race. Math performance declined in the former and rose in the latter; subsequent work showed that levels of activity in

cortical brain regions involved in math skills shifted in opposite directions as well. (Shih, Pittinsky, & Ambady, 1999; Harada, Bridge, Chia, 2013). As another example, recall that the fusiform cortex activates more, and recall of the face is more accurate, when subjects look at a same- versus different-race face. In one study, subjects were mixed-raced individuals, and when cued beforehand to identify with one of the two races, the accuracy of their memory for faces of that race improved (Van Bavel & Cunningham, 2009).

Implicit in us belonging to multiple in-groups is that each comes with its own distinctive out-group. The fact that the relative importance of particular Us/Them dichotomies can shift means that the same person can count as an out-group member in one setting, and in-group in another. In a quiet way, this is the single most important and hopeful fact in this review.

This recategorization has been shown experimentally concerning race. In one study, American subjects where shown a series of either black or white faces, each associated with a quote; subjects were supposed to remember which quote went with which face. There was automatic categorization of faces by race, shown by the fact that if a quote was mis-attributed, it was likely to be of someone of the same race as the actual individual. Yet, if half the faces of each race where pictured wearing a yellow shirt, half in a grey one, automatic categorization shifted to being predominately by shirt color. (Kurzban, Tooby, & Cosmides, 2001) Another example concerns the typical activation of the amygdala by another-race face. However, such activation does not occur if the other-race face is of a beloved celebrity; in such cases, their fame makes them more of an Us than their race makes them a Them (Kubota, Banaji, & Phelps, 2012). Another studies shows that it is easier to condition a fear response to an other-race face than to a same-race face, so long as the faces are male; if female, gender categorization outweighs racial categorization (Navarrete et al., 2009).

Similar recategorization occurs in the real world. For example, a Shiite Iranian might view an Iraqi as a Them, thanks to traditional Persian/Mesopotamian rivalry. But when it comes to denominational religious tensions, that Shiite Iraqi might now count as an Us, when compared to a Saudi Arabian Sunni. And if the dichotomy that dominates is the "clash of civilizations" analysis of contemporary cultural conflicts, that Saudi becomes an Us, when compared to an American fundamentalist Christian.

Remarkably, such recategorization can occur in circumstances of the most severe, hate-filled inter-group conflict. In the American Civil War of the 1860s, men on opposite sides were known to aid each other if they recognized secret signs indicating that they were both Freemasons (Halleran, 2010), or if the green sprigs intentionally placed in their hats indicated that they were both Irish-American (Kennealy, 2000). During World War II, in a life-or-death situation, a British officer and his prisoner, a German officer, shifted categories into something resembling a friendship that lasted decades when they discovered by chance that they shared a love of Greek classics (Leigh Fermor, 2014). And in perhaps the most famous example, during the first Christmas of World War I, in 1914, what was meant to be a three-hour truce for retrieval of the dead from between the trenches, turned into multiple days of enemy soldiers sharing meals and gifts, singing, praying and playing football together, and making pacts to shoot over each other's heads when they were forced by the powers that be behind the lines to return to fighting (Weintraub, 2002). Thus, in the least auspicious of circumstances, an in-/out-group distinction built around bloodied nationalism evaporated, replaced by a shared sense of identity among soldiers on both sides of the line with the most to lose in a war.

Conclusions
Each species is unique. Nonetheless, some are arguably unique

in more unique ways; this certainly pertains to our own species. The least unique thing concerning the biology of pro- and anti-social behavior in humans is that our Us/Them dichotomizing is built heavily around neurobiology that is rapid, implicit, automatic, and affective. The most unique thing is how that ancient neurobiology is then harnessed in the service of the most astonishingly abstract dichotomies, ones that can be displaced over vast time and space. We can weep for someone living a thousand miles away, or hate someone for what their ancestors did a thousand years ago.

The adverse consequences of the unique ways in which we distinguish between in- and out-group members permeates our lives. It has certainly motivated my own interest in this subject. I grew up in a relatively tough neighborhood in New York City, one with considerable tension, even violence, built along ethnic, religious and racial lines. Adding to that, I then spent more than thirty summers studying wild baboons in southwestern Kenya and, in the process, got to observe similar tensions between the neighboring Masai and surrounding Kipsigi and Kuria communities (not to mention observing the consequences of the 2007-2008 Kenyan election catastrophe). These two realms of in-group/out-group conflict, at other ends of the planet, had far more commonalities than differences, and it is hard not to be left pessimistic.

Despite that, there are grounds for optimism. While it seems hard-wired that we automatically make Us/Them distinctions, we are vastly malleable as to which ones we make, and the same cortical processes that make us pseudo-speciate an enemy into seeming sub-human explains the potential for pseudo-kinship with ex-enemies. Moreover, there has been considerable progress in understanding the processes that give rise to such changes (Sapolsky, 2017). Inter-group tensions can be reduced on behavioral, affective and even neurobiological levels by techniques such as perspective-taking, individuating out-group members out of being mere faceless Thems, and prolonged contact under specific, narrow circumstances (where individuals from both sides come together in roughly equal numbers in a neutral setting and with strongly motivated shared goals). The human capacity for abstraction has fueled no shortage of bloodshed of types unique to our species; fortunately, it can fuel the opposite as well.

References

Altmann, J. (2001) *Baboon mothers and infants*. Chicago, IL: University of Chicago Press.

Bartal, I., Decety, J., Mason, P. (2011) *Empathy and pro-social behavior in rats*. Science, 334, 1427.

Batson, C. (1987) Prosocial motivation: Is it ever truly altruistic? Advances in *Experimental and Social Psychology*, 20, 65.

Creel, S., Creel, N. M. *The African Wild Dog: Behavior, Ecology, and Conservation:* Princeton, NJ, Princeton University Press.

Cunningham, W., Nezlek, J., Banaji, M. (2004) Implicit and explicit ethnocentrism: Revisiting the ideologies of prejudice. *Personality and Social Psychology Bulletin*, 30, 1332.

de Waal, F. B. M. (2007) *Chimpanzee Politics: Power and Sex Among Apes*. Baltimore, MD: Johns Hopkins University Press.

de Waal, F. B. M., Preston, S. (2017) Mammalian empathy: behavioural manifestations and neural basis. *Nature Reviews Neuroscience*. 18, 498.

Feinstein, J., Adolphs, R., Damasio, A., Tranel, D (2011) The human amygdala and the induction and experience of fear. *Current Biology*, 21, 34

Fiske, S., Cuddy, J., Glick, P., Xu, J. (2002) A model of (often mixed) stereotype content: Competence and warmth respectively follow from perceived status and competition. *Journal of Personality and Social Psychology*, 82, 878.

Golby, A., Gabrieli, J., Chiao, J., Eberhardt, J. (2001) Differential responses in the fusiform region to same-race and other-race faces. *Nature Neuroscience*, 4, 845.

Goodall, J. (2010) *In the Shadow of Man.* Wilmington, DE: Mariner Books.

Haidt, J. (2012) *The Righteous Mind: Why Good People are Divided by Politics and Religion.* New York, NY: Pantheon Books.

Haidt, J. (2001) The emotional dog and its rational tail: A social intuitionist approach to moral judgment. *Psychological Review,* 108, 814.

Halleran, M. (2010) *The Better Angels of Our Nature: Freemasonry in the American Civil War.* Tuscaloosa, AL: The University of Alabama Press, 2010.

Harada, T., Bridge, D., Chiao, J. (2013) Dynamic social power modulates neural basis of math calculation. *Frontiers of Human Neuroscience,* 6, 350.

Harris, L., Fiske, S. (2006) Dehumanizing the lowest of the low: neuroimaging responses to extreme out-groups. *Psychological Science,* 17, 847.

Harris, L., Fiske, T. (2007) Social groups that elicit disgust are differentially processed in *mPFC. SCAN,* 2, 45.

Hart, A., Whalen, P., Shin, L., McInerney, S., Fischer, H., Rauch, S. (2000) Differential response in the human amygdala to racial outgroup versus ingroup face stimuli. *Neuroreport,* 11, 2351.

Haruno, M., Frith, C. (2010) Activity in the amygdala elicited by unfair divisions predicts social value orientation. *Nature Neuroscience,* 13, 160.

Hausfater G., Hrdy S.B. (1984) *Infanticide. Comparative and Evolutionary Perspectives.* New York, NY: Aldine.

Hermans, E., Ramsey, N., von Honk, J. (2008) Exogenous testosterone enhances responsiveness to social threat in the neural circuitry of social aggression in humans. *Biological Psychiatry,* 63, 263.

Jacob, S., McLintock, M., Zelano, B., Ober, C. (2002) Paternally inherited HLA alleles are associated with women's choice of male odor. *Nature Genetics* 30, 175.

Kendrick, K., Drewett, R. (1979) Testosterone reduces refractory period of stria terminalis neurons in the rat brain. *Science,* 204,

877.

Kennealy, T. (2000) *The Great Shame: And the Triumph of the Irish in the English-Speaking World.* New York, NY: Anchor Books.

Kubota, J., Banaji, M., Phelps, E. (2012) *The neuroscience of race. Nature Neuroscience*, 15, 940.

Kurzban, R., Tooby, J., Cosmides, L. (2001) Can race be erased? Coalitional computation and social categorization. *Proceedings of the National Academy of Sciences USA*, 98, 15387.

Langford, D., Crager, S., Shehzad, Z., Smith, S., Sotocinal, S., Levenstadt, J., Chanda, M., Levitin,D.,Mogil, J. (2006) *Social modulation of pain as evidence for empathy in mice. Science*, 312, 1967.

LeDoux, J. (1998) *The Emotional Brain: The Mysterious Underpinnings of Emotional Life.* New York, NY: Simon Schuster.

Leigh Fermor, P. (2014). *Abducting a General: The Kreipe Operation and SOE in Crete.* London, UK: John Murray.

Maestripieri D. (2007) *Machiavellian Intelligence: How Rhesus Macaques and Humans Have Conquered the World.* Chicago, IL: University of Chicago Press.

Mahajan, N., Martinez, M., Gutierrez, N., Diesendruck, G., Banaji, M., Santos, L. (2011) The evolution of intergroup bias: perceptions and attitudes in rhesus macaques. *Journal of Personality and Social Psychology* 100, 387.

Mitchell, J., Nosek, B., Banaji, M. (2003) Contextual variations in implicit evaluation. *Journal of Experimental Psychology: General,* 132, 455.

Mogil, J. (2012) The surprising empathic abilities of rodents. *Trends in Cognitive Sciences,* 16, 143.

Morris, M. W., Podolny, J. M., Ariel, S. 2000. Missing relations: Incorporating relational constructs into models of culture. In Earley, P. C. & Singh, H. (Eds.), *Innovations in international and cross cultural management*: 52–90. Thousand Oaks, CA: Sage.

Navarrete, C., Olsson, A., Ho, A., Mendes, W., Thomsen, L.,Sidanius, J. (2009) Fear extinction to an out-group face: the role of target gender. *Psychological Science*, 20, 155.

Niebuhr R, (1941) *The Nature and Destiny of Man (Vol. 1).* London,

UK: Nisbet & Company.

Nosek, B., Hawkins, C., Frazier, R. (2011) Implicit social cognition: from measures to mechanisms. *Trends in Cognitive Sciences,* 15, 152.

Peterson, D., Wrangham, R. (1997) *Demonic Males: Apes and the Origins of Human Violence.* Wilmington, DE: Mariner.

Rice, G., Gainer, P. (1962) "Altruism" in the albino rat. *Journal of Comparative and Physiological Psychology,* 55, 123.

Rodrigues, S., LeDoux, J., Sapolsky, R. (2009) The influence of stress hormones on fear circuitry. *Annual Review of Neuroscience,* 32. 289.

Sanfey, A., Rilling, J., Aronson, J., Nystrom, L., Cohen, J. (2003) The neural basis of economic decision-making in the Ultimatum Game. *Science* 300, 1755.

Sapolsky, R. (2001) *A Primate's Memoir.* New York, NY: Scribner.

Sapolsky, R. (2017) *Behave: The Biology of Humans at Our Best and Worst.* New York, NY: Penguin Books.

Shepher, J. (1971) Mate selection among second generation kibbutz adolescents and adults: incest avoidance and negative imprinting. *Archives of Sexual Behavior,* 1, 293.

Shih, M., Pittinsky, T., Ambady, N. (1999) Stereotype susceptibility: identity salience and shifts in quantitative performance. *Psychological Science,* 10, 80.

Tajfel, H. (1970) Experiments in intergroup discrimination. *Scientific American,* 223, 96.

Tajfel, H., (1982) Social psychology of intergroup relations. *Annual Review of Psychology* 33, 1.

Van Bavel, J., Cunningham, W. (2009) Self-categorization with a novel mixed-race group moderates automatic social and racial biases. *Personality and Social Psychology Bulletin,* 35, 321.

Weintraub, S. (2002) *Silent Night: The Story of the World War I Christmas Truce.* New York, NY: Plume Press.

Zald, D. (2003) The human amygdala and the emotional evaluation of sensory stimuli. *Brain Research Reviews,* 41, 88.

ETHNIC AND RACIAL CONFLICT FROM RELIGIOUS POINT OF VIEW
GLEN T. MARTIN

Conflicting Philosophies

In mature religion, the whole includes the holism of humanity but goes beyond it to the whole of the divine Ground of Existence.

Today, conflict seems to be everywhere. Human communities worldwide struggle within their local environments, which include local cultural, economic, and political conditions. However, globalized economics, transportation, and information systems also place peoples around the globe within a planetary environment in which events that happen elsewhere in the world have a greater or lesser impact on immediate conditions. The availability of lethal weapons everywhere on Earth also increases the prospects for deadly conflict. Ethnic, racial, and group conflicts can be exacerbated or mitigated by local, regional, and global conditions. Conflict often arises because our world is globalized while our religious, cultural, and group perspectives remain localized and parochial.

In a world where the news coming to us from around the globe is often frightening and deeply disturbing, we often cling all the more firmly to our local group, culture, religion, and identity. Yet this act of exclusive identification may itself exacerbate racial or ethnic conflict with other groups who are similarly embracing their exclusive identities to the exclusion of others. We need to discover strategies and paradigms that encourage active peace processes everywhere on Earth directed toward expanding our perspectives to global and even cosmic dimensions.

This essay argues that over the past century human beings have reached a globalized understanding of religion that bears directly on how we address our conflicts with one another. It argues that this new emergent understanding of religion and our human condition can contribute a great deal to our ability to address our conflicts and establish peace with our neighbors at the local, regional, and global levels. To understand religion deeply, along with its implications as to how we should live our lives within our smaller and larger communities, can contribute immensely to solving our conflicts, reconciling with one another, and establishing enduring peace.

In spite of this emerging civilizational awareness, human beings entered into the 21st century from a 20th century that exhibited a shameful record for human history. Our shameful record is revealed through such books as Jonathan Glover's Humanity: A Moral History of the 20th Century or Evelin Lindner's Making Enemies: Humiliation and International Conflict. Such books detail the horrors of wars, torture, genocides, and perversions that have characterized our inhumanity to one another during the past century. When brought into focus within single books such as these, our human condition may look hopeless and bleak, indeed.

Even apart from the detailed historical record, most of us

are familiar with many current racial and ethnic conflicts today. To name just a few: the oppression of blacks in the USA, Hindu-Moslem conflicts in India, men humiliating women in Afghanistan, Saudi Arabia, and elsewhere. The list continues apparently without end: Shiites versus Sunnis, repression of gays in Russia, repression of Baha'is in Iran, the Israeli-Palestinian conflict, the genocide and displacement of the Rohingya people in Myanmar, on-going Christian-Moslem conflict in Bosnia and Macedonia, anti-immigrant sentiments in European countries, tribal conflicts many places in Africa, and the abandonment of the Hispanic population of Puerto Rico after Hurricane Maria by the racist "white supremacist" government of the US.

We begin with conflicting identities, painful histories, and a past of accusations, perceived injustices, and traumatic memories. In our interdependent world, we realize that we might all live more securely, peacefully, and fully if we were interacting in cooperation, rather than conflict, with our neighbors. What are the ways forward by which we can transform conflicts without compromising our values, identities, and loyalties?

How can we enlarge our identities to truly reconcile with the other without giving up our distinct, embodied sense of who we are? How can we create unity in diversity rather than remaining in the fragmentation of an unredeemed situation of conflict? All of these questions bear on the question of the new paradigm for being human that has emerged during the past century. And this new paradigm has much to do with the deeper understanding of religion that has also emerged over the past century. Toward the end of this essay, I will address some concrete proposals and processes for dealing with ethnic and racial conflict proposed by people active in this field. First, let us examine the nature of religion.

1. Emergence of religious maturity in human civilization

Beginning toward the end of the 19th century, quality

translations of the basic scriptures of the world's religions began to become available. For the first time it was possible to study each religion in a scholarly way rather than simply try to understand it though hearsay or secondary sources. In the same period, scholarship became more sophisticated in that it began to understand each religion as conditioned by its historical development, and not, therefore, locked in stone as a timeless set of dogmas or beliefs.

Most of the historical, critical scholarship of religious texts and traditions that has developed since that time has been done by religious thinkers and believers themselves, not by secularists or atheists. Such scholars have pointed out, for example, that in the Christian New Testament God, like God's incarnation in Jesus as the Christ, is identified with Truth. The Prologue to the Gospel of John proclaims "In the beginning was the Logos, and the Logos was with God, and the Logos was God." The word logos is often translated into English as "Word": "In the beginning was the Word." The meaning here refers to the "divine reason" or "creative order" at the heart of the world. Jesus proclaims that He is "the truth and the light," and the Gospel of John understands this truth and light as the source of all being and creation: "All things were made by him; and without him was not any thing made that was made."

For the Greek and Roman fathers of the Christian faith, the logos in us, our ability to think carefully and discern the structures of what was made (the world), is fundamental to our being made in the image of God. Human reason, intelligence, and discernment of the truth are God's image in us and gift to us. Today, historical critical scholarship of religious texts is a reflection of this gift.

In the Vedic tradition of India, the highest reality is Brahman or God, characterized as sat, chit, and ananda. Sat means being, and from this root comes satya, meaning truth, truthfulness, or reality. God is being (truth), consciousness (intelligence), and bliss (joy), and our soul (Atman) can realize this being, consciousness and bliss through a properly lived human life. Mahatma Gandhi (the "great souled" one) made the goal of his life and action satyagraha, literally "clinging to truth" (see Jesudasan 1984). When one clings to truth in this way, "no one and nothing is a stranger to me" (De Martino 1960, 127).

If God is truth, if God is truly the foundation of the creative order and meaning of the universe, then researching the truth cannot harm us; it can only liberate us. The pursuit of truth (mandated and gifted to us by God), may end up challenging our naïve religious assumptions, our interpretive narrowness, or our intransigent, blind dogmatisms. If God really is truth, then this is all to the good. God's greatness is not threatened by the pursuit of truth, by moral and intellectual integrity regarding truth. Just the opposite; if God really is truth, the more truth that human beings discover, the closer they come to God.

It is the same with love. The Christian New Testament, like many other scriptures around the world, proclaims that God is love (agape), and that God's love for us (agape) is unconditional, just as our love for one another (agape) must be unconditional. However, if this is the case, we need not be critical or suspicious of people who love and advocate love without mentioning God. If God is really love, then the more love there is in the world the closer the world comes to God. As Raimon Panikkar puts this on behalf of the "advaitic love" of the Indian Vedantas: "I love you with an inclusive and unique love, which is the current of universal love that passes through you, as it were, for in my love of you universal love is kindled and finds its expression" (1979, 285).

It is the same with truth, the more people pursue truth (whether or not they mention God), the closer the world is to God, for God is both truth and love. All finite and relative truths participate in the Absolute Truth. A mature relationship with both truth and love is therefore a mature relationship with God.

In my 2005 book, *Millennium Dawn*, I identified several developments since the 19th century that interface with critical research concerning traditional religious texts and the history of the world's religions. The first of these is historical and critical scholarship itself. The second involves the realization that all social and natural phenomena are historical or evolutionary in character. There appear to be no ahistorical realities available to human knowledge. Even universal moral principles get reinterpreted with respect to historical time and circumstances. Therefore, traditional religious texts that appear to be revealing timeless truths need to be reinterpreted as historical documents pointing beyond themselves to the Ground of Being or God. They must be understood as historicized documents subject to interpretation and reinterpretation as human beings continue to grow toward intellectual, moral, and religious maturity.

Third, these insights necessarily lead to a process of "demythologization" of traditional religious beliefs so that we are able to separate antiquated cosmologies and belief systems from the essential spiritual, ethical, and soteriological messages contained in these texts. Fourth, with the emergence of excellent translations of world religious texts since the late 19th century, the study of comparative religion has completely transformed our naïve ethnocentric preferences regarding our own religious texts compared to "inferior" and "heathen" foreign texts. It turns out that there are profound similarities in the religious experiences, concepts, and theologies of peoples worldwide.

Fifth, the systematic comparative study of "mysticism," as recorded in the testimonies of religious persons worldwide, shows an astonishing similarity of these fundamental experiences that are at the heart of every religious tradition. Books such as Rudolph Otto's *Mysticism East and West*, F.C. Happold's *Religious Faith & Twentieth-Century Man*, Elmer O'Brien's *Varieties of Mystic Experience,* and Water Stace's *Mysticism and Philosophy* helped pave the way for a flood of scholarly literature testifying to the sameness and depth of human spirituality and religious experience everywhere on Earth.

Finally, there has been a convergence of all these developments, which interface to liberate human beings toward discerning the truth of our human situation with regard to religion and spirituality. A host of profound scholars and thinkers have been working to develop and articulate a universal theology of religions: thinkers as diverse as Fritjof Schuon in his *Transcendent Unity of Religions*, Hans Küng in his *Theology for the Third Millennium*, and David J. Krieger in his *The New Universalism: Foundations for a Global Theology*.

As a result of these worldwide scholarly endeavors, many sacred texts were discovered to be composites of documents written at different times by different authors. Secondly, the religious texts themselves began to be understood in terms of the languages, cultures, and customs of the times within which they were written, and not, therefore, as timeless pronouncements from a transcendent deity requiring no interpretation and no understanding of the contexts in which they were produced. Thoughtful people began to understand the relativity and contingency of religious beliefs.

Throughout the 20th century, numerous studies of comparative religion were produced showing the astonishing similarities of religious experiences and beliefs worldwide and revealing cultural, linguistic, and territorial differences as secondary to these broad patterns. The first World Parliament of Religions took place in 1893 at the Art Institute in Chicago, bringing together leaders from the world's great religions in dialogue directed toward mutual understanding. Since that time, there have been four more meetings of the World Parliament, the last one in 2015 and the next scheduled for 2018. Inter-faith dialogue has become a major focus of this movement and many other organizations. The idea of the exclusive "truth" of any one religion implying that all the other religions are false has largely disappeared from thoughtful people worldwide.

2. Stages of religious maturity versus immaturity

Coming out of this tradition, professor of religions James Fowler (1981) defined six stages in the development of faith-maturity. He called the simple belief stage of preschool children "Intuitive-Projective." Once children become socialized into their faith communities, they enter the "Mythic-Literal" stage in which they accept ideas of their community as the truth and take them literally. As children grow into the teen years, they will often move into the "Synthetic-Conventional" stage of religious maturity. Since by now they have often experienced a few differing faith orientations from the various communities they have encountered, they develop a larger synthetic belief system to account for all these variations. However, they do not realize that their larger system itself remains a limited belief system.

In young adulthood, people may encounter the vast variety of authentic belief systems in the world and become skeptics, realizing that their own former belief system was limited and one of many possible systems. Sometime in mid-life, Fowler suggests, people may develop a fifth stage: "Conjunctive Faith." They begin to encounter the deeper mysteries of life and begin to understand that faith systems symbolize these deeper mysteries. At this stage of faith, they may return to the belief system in which they were raised; however, now without being trapped in the belief that it is the final truth and all other systems are merely illusory.

The highest stage (stage 6), Fowler calls "Universalizing Faith." It is here that people, no matter what their faith orientation, realize the heart and soul that is at the core of all the great faiths of the world:

In their devotion to universalizing compassion, they may offend our parochial conceptions of justice. In their penetration through the obsession with survival, security, and significance they threaten our measured standards of righteousness and goodness and prudence. Their enlarged versions of universal community disclose the partialness of our tribes and pseudo-species.... They have become incarnators and actualizers of the spirit of an inclusive and fulfilled human community. They are contagious in the sense that they create zones of liberation from the social, political, economic, and ideological shackles we place and endure on human futurity. (1981, 200-201)

Here we have a characterization of the most mature, highest, stage of religious growth and self-actualization. People have incarnated the truths of their religious backgrounds to the point where they no longer "believe in" love, truth, or justice, or the literal truth of their scriptures, but become living embodiments of the love and truth that are also identified with God.

In *An Interpretation of Religion,* John Hick argues that this self-realization toward becoming a living embodiment of love and truth serves as a criterion by which we recognize a true "saint" or embodiment of the Word of God (2004, Chaps. 17 & 18). He quotes extensively from Confucian, Taoist, Buddhist, Hindu, Zoroastrian, Christian, Jewish, and Moslem texts to show the universality of this claim. As people grow to religious maturity, they first see that the Truth of the universe transcends all particular religious embodiments of that Truth. They see that all the great religions are different paths up the same mountain toward God, Brahman, Allah, or the Dharmakaya of Buddhism.

If they continue to grow toward becoming living embodiments of the love and truth represented by these prophets and saints, they begin living as described by James Fowler: "They have identified their community as all humanity and revealed the partial nature of our limited identities in terms of "our tribes and pseudo-species." They have become authentic representatives of a fulfilled and flourishing human community. This growth is natural in us in the sense that religious maturity fulfills our lives with mature meaning, wisdom, and purpose, and opens us to a universal compassion for all others persons and the Earth's other living creatures.

By contrast, in those whose growth process is stunted and incomplete, their need for fulfilled meaning and purpose is correspondingly derailed. They succumb to neurotic and often fanatical forms of smallness and rigidity. Philosopher and psychologist Eric Fromm identifies them as "neurotic," a condition in which they fixate on "a private form of religion" to compensate for their "failure...to accomplish the fundamental aims of human existence, independence, and the ability to be productive, to love, to think" (1950, Chap. 3).

Religion is not most fundamentally these rituals, songs, or practices. It is not these myths or stories, for they are all merely the means by which we ascend toward truth and love. They are the means by which we participate in the divine Ground of Being, in the worship and reality of God. Religion is the divine spirit operating in our hearts and minds moving us toward reconciliation, forgiveness, mutual respect, understanding, love, compassion, inclusiveness, and distributive, all-embracing justice.

From about the mid-twentieth century, psychologists and philosophers began to arrive at a consensus concerning human growth and development. They were able to define stages of emotional, cognitive, religious, and ethical growth toward maturity. Thinkers who participate in this broad consensus include James Fowler, Eric Fromm, Carol Gilligan, Jürgen Habermas, Lawrence Kohlberg, Abraham Maslow, Jean Piaget, and Ken Wilber. Kolhberg (1984), for example, described seven broad stages in cognitive development that may be simplified into an early egoistic stage, moving to an ethnocentric stage, then to a worldcentric maturity, and beyond to a kosmocentric maturity (that he called "stage seven").

In contrast with such maturity, philosopher and theologian

Paul Tillich describes the "literalism" characteristic of fundamentalist religious orientations that operates to deny and block the growth process toward human maturity:

> *Literalism deprives God of his ultimacy and, religiously speaking, of his majesty. It draws him down to the level of that which us not ultimate, the finite and conditional. In the last analysis it is not rational criticism of the myth which is decisive but the inner religious criticism. Faith, if it takes its symbols literally, becomes idolatrous! It calls something ultimate which is less than ultimate. Faith, conscious of the symbolic character of its symbols, gives God the honor which is due him. (1957, 52).*

Fundamentalist and literalist religions worship a false, "idolatrous" God because they worship the textual and ritual manifestations rather than the living God toward which these point. As Fromm points out, thwarted growth toward maturity results in neurosis, irrationality, and self-induced blindness.

3. The question of religion versus spirituality

Some authors speak of religion that is free of mythic images (Ferré 1982). Others speak of "spirituality" as distinct from religion (Agnivesh 2015). Still others may speak of the dynamics of "faith" as opposed to specific religious beliefs (Tillich 1957). In all of these cases, these linguistic distinctions appear to be a matter of semantics, a matter of how we want to use the words "religion, spirituality, and faith," rather than substantive issues. Nevertheless, the insight that I developed above remains fundamental: the literal, textual claims found in all the world's scriptures, point beyond themselves to the living reality of Truth and Love and therefore, as literal stories and statements, constitute a "mythos" that must be understood as such. We must see beyond the texts to the living God.

Philosopher of religion, Friedrich Ferré, for example, points out the ways in which each particular religious mythos may limit the individual from authentic religious growth: "a person's religion is not constituted first of all by his allegiance to imagery but rather by his most comprehensive and intensive valuations." Through authentic religious growth, we can achieve "a wholeness that is always open, a unity that, by its very nature, is hospitable to growth - this is what is needed as the basis for religious maturity and life's fullest integrity" (1982, 349-51). Embracing a single religious tradition with literalism or fundamentalism can cut us off from the holism of a truly world-embracing process of growth.

Ferré asks how we free ourselves "from the parochialism of association and imagination that ties us to the mythos of a single community" that "no longer seems quite large enough for life" (ibid., 345). Our religious inwardness (sometimes called "spirituality") deepens as we see our sacred texts as pointing us to the Ground of Being (God) in which we participate through growing evermore fully into truth and love. Ferré affirms that: "We need a revitalized sense of mystery in knowing. At best our cognitive constructs are only that: cognitive constructs. The better they are the more they reveal the mysteries beyond" (ibid., 346). The most basic point of all the great religions is perhaps the need for incarnation of the spirit of Truth and Love into our own lives.

Those who have reached Fowler's stage five of religious maturity begin to understand that we need not embrace one of these symbols-systems to the exclusion of others. Human religious maturity grows toward the Truth and Love of God independently of any particular cultural mythology that we may adopt. Any particular mythology may itself impose unneeded limitations on our capacity for growth. As S. Radikrishnan puts this in his exposition of the *Bhagavad Gita*:

By developing our inner spiritual nature, we gain a new kind of relatedness to the world and grow in freedom, where the integrity of the self is not compromised. We then become aware of ourselves as active creative individuals, living, not by the discipline of external authority but by the inward rule of free devotion to truth. (1973, 44-45)

This call can itself form the basis for a religious life, independent of any or all traditional mythologies. Through authentic religious participation, we can achieve a holism hospitable to authentic growth and integrity. One danger with embracing a specific traditional religious mythology is that it can limit the holism of a truly world-embracing process of growth.

Just as religious maturity has been rapidly spreading in human civilization since the quality translation work of the late nineteenth century, so we have seen that psychology has been presenting a vision of human maturity grounded in the holism of our situation. We are one human species living on one, small planet, with a tremendous biological, psychological, and civilizational unity that manifests itself through a wide diversity of cultures, races, nation-states, and religions. The reality of our universe and our human situation is unity in diversity, not a fragmented and atomized diversity; we are all the same.

These breakthroughs of the 20th century have been complemented by the natural sciences. Since Einstein's special theory of relativity was published in 1905, continuing through present advances in quantum physics, the universe has been understood to be a holistic and unified system of fields within fields manifesting diversity through its astonishing integrated unity. Natural science, social science, theories of language and culture - all point to the fundamental reality of holism manifesting itself in a unity in diversity in which the diversity does not exist and could not exist apart from the whole (see Bohm 1980; Capra 1996).

There is an organization on-line called "Boundary-less World" at www.boundaryless.net. They bring interested persons into a process of increased self-awareness and transformative growth through showing that our divisions and separations from one another are located primarily in our minds, not in some imagined "external realities." Their program reveals the arbitrary character of all our so-called boundaries:

> The question boils down to "what do we honor most?' What do we honor more than a human being? Is it "caste, creed, faith, religion, belief, values, ideology, lifestyle, food habits, color, beauty, nationality, ethnicity, age, gender, martial status, sexual preferences, profession, economic status, merit, knowledge, wisdom, health, strength," etc. Each of these value judgements creates a boundary between us and other human beings. The question is what do we love most? Do we value other human beings most or do we value the boundaries? Each boundary that we cling to or identify with (say race, gender, or nationality), they say, establishes a prison and each hardened boundary is a source of conflict. (Ibid.)

> To really love other human beings we must love them without boundaries. We must value them as human beings first rather than as members of some group defined by artificial boundaries. Through a process of dialogue and self-examination one can become ever-more aware of the immense number of artificial boundaries that one imposes upon the world and on relationships. (Ibid.)

This dovetails with authentic religion as I have been defining it. At the highest stages of religious growth, human beings become "incarnators and actualizers of the spirit of an inclusive and fulfilled human community," which means a community without boundaries. Swami Agnivesh writes:

> The business of true spirituality, in the end, is for love to supersede power as the shaping paradigm for the human species. The essence of the spiritual light that all great religious seers have brought is the need for the human species to shift from the love of power to the power of love. Compassion, fellow feeling, selfless commitment to an altruistic cause, the spirit of sacrificial service, social justice,

and respect for human worth and human equality are all authentic
expressions of the power of love - whereas the love of power sees them
either as superfluous or as liabilities. (2015, 68)

All the great religious seers have underlined the power of love.
Like Jesus in the Gospels, who associated with prostitutes, with
the despised Samaritans, and other non-Jews (with all kinds of
people who were discriminated against by the religious leaders
of his day) so today, those of mature religion "are contagious
in the sense that they create zones of liberation from the social,
political, economic, and ideological shackles we place and endure
on human futurity." Love and Truth know no boundaries.
The social, political, economic, and ideological shackles (the
myths, rituals, and parochial loyalties) serve as boundaries
discriminating these human beings from those - my race, my
religion, and my ethnicity from yours. Mahatma Gandhi's
religion was that of satyagraha (clinging to truth). This allowed
him to embrace all religions, all differences, and all persons in
his undiscriminating love.

Religious maturity need not abandon loyalty to this or that
religious framework. I may remain a Christian or Moslem or
Hindu. But I have discovered that God is love and that authentic
love is boundary-less. It is directed toward persons as such, not
to persons of this or that race, religion, or nation. The divine
Ground of Being does not demand from us that we remain
loyal to this or that religious identity: that I am a Christian, or
Moslem, or Hindu. What is demanded is love and truth, and
transformation to actions based on love and truth, not on actions
based on separations, differences, and parochial identities.

4. Nation-state fragmentation versus the holism of our world system

Something similar can be said regarding the ideas of human
dignity and human rights that have developed widely since the
20th century and articulated in a powerful form in the 1948 UN

Universal Declaration of Human Rights. Chapter two of my recent book *Human Transcendence and Our Global Social Contract* discusses the grounds for the concept of human dignity at some length. Suffice it here to say that human self-awareness and freedom opens up a dimension of "infinity" within our humanity that is incommensurable with all price or material calculations of value or disvalue. As such, dignity, or the privilege of being an end in oneself (intrinsically valuable simply by existing as oneself), applies only to human beings, not to groups, cultures, or nations. In other words, human dignity and human rights transcend culture, nationality, and all human-made boundaries.

Human rights scholar Jack Donnelly cites Ann-Belinda Preis in what he calls "the most important article on culture and human rights published in the 1990s." Preis concludes, he says, that anthropologists have come to a broad consensus that there is no such thing as a culture that is "a homogeneous, integral, and coherent unity." All cultures are fluid, dynamic "complexes of intersubjective meanings and practices" (2003, 86) Especially in today's interacting, interdependent world, every culture is continually in the process of transition and subject to innumerable influences negative and positive.

Something very similar can be said of nation-states, despite the fact that nation-states have fixed territorial borders. Benedict Anderson studied the way national identities have been formed in his book *Imagined Communities: Reflections on the Origin and Spread of Nationalism (2006)*. Governments of nation-states rule over a variety of languages, cultures, ethnicities, races, religions, and ideologies. It is an illusion to speak of a national community or a national set of values that somehow intrinsically adhere to this or that nation.

As governments try to cobble together a sense of national identity in order to attract recruits to their militaries or motivate citizens to public service, minorities often feel oppressed in these circumstances and arbitrary appeals to "patriotism" rarely succeed in wielding national groupings into coherent communities. As Jorge M. Valadez states, "Nation-states cannot claim to have a morally unconditional claim on their territories, for they generally acquired them through violent conquest, invasive settlement, broken treaties, and other morally illegitimate means" (2008, 266). As 18th century philosopher Immanuel Kant points out, the idea that nations have "rights" is often linked to their supposed "right" to make war, which is self-contradictory, since what is "right" cannot be protected and decided by what is wrong (i.e., by the victory of mere power rather than rational principles) (1983, 116-17).

The human community is our fundamental reality, not nation-states, which, like our cultures and religious identities, will forever remain arbitrary and historically contingent. And our human community is made up of individual human beings who are the sole bearers of inalienable rights and dignity. Nations do not have such rights, nor do cultures or groups. Such collectivities may have legitimacy and assigned privileges. For example, the government of California may have legitimacy as assigned to it by the Constitution of the USA. It may have the "right" or privilege to collect taxes from its citizens, but this is a different sense of the word "right" from that which applies to the human rights of citizens. It is not "inalienable" and it is not derived from the infinite worth or dignity of the state of California.

A deep understanding of the historical contingency of nation-states points forward to a *Constitution for the Federation of Earth* that is premised on our human universality of dignity, rights, and the need for peace and sustainability on our planet (www.earth-constitution.org). The Preamble to this *Earth Constitution* states that "unity in diversity is the basis for a new age when war shall be outlawed and peace prevail; when the Earth's total resources shall be equitably used for human welfare; and when basic human rights and responsibilities shall be shared by all without discrimination" (see Martin 2010). Nation states form arbitrary and ultimately unreal boundaries between peoples just as much as do religions, races, and classes. Understanding the essence of religion, or the essence of human rights, points forward to a democratic Earth Federation embracing all citizens of the Earth. Let us turn our attention, then, to the ways that the peace process reflects and embodies these principles.

5. Strategies for reconciliation: unity in diversity

5.1. In all cases the practitioners and theorists of an ethnic or racial peace process emphasize the need for a self-aware, intentionally followed process. And in all cases, these peace thinkers emphasize the need for finding a larger framework of common interests and values that allow the conflicted parties to enter into the process of solidifying a relationship based on these larger premises. It should be clear that the above description of authentic religion and human rights provides what may be the largest possible framework: the wholeness of humanity under God, and the unique dignity of each of us.

In her book *Roadmap to Reconciliation: Moving Communities into Unity, Wholeness, and Justice,* Brenda Salter McNeil approaches the peace process in the light of Jesus' emphasis on the kind of peaceful and flourishing communities and societies we should strive to create. She emphasizes stages in a process that are collectively developed and followed by the conflicting parties. The process often begins with "catalytic events" that bring a simmering conflict to light and make people understand that reconciliation is necessary.

The participants must ensure an "ongoing interaction environment" that is "inherent in every phase of the process" (2015, 37). She identifies stages in the path as realization, identification, preparation, and activation. In the stage of realization, people begin to understand that they are "contextually connected." The conflicting parties intentionally enter into a dialogue that explores the issues, connections, and contexts of their perceptions, resentments, and actions. Out of this comes perception of a "new reality" that makes the situation look quite different from the initial viewpoints of the conflicting parties.

From the realization process, through common efforts the groups can move to the "identification phase," which "is where we begin to identify with and relate to other people who are experiencing the same thing" (2015, 66). Our cultural identity begins to shift, and our assumptions about how we should relate to each other shift to the point where reconciliation can begin to occur (ibid., 68). From here groups can move to the "preparation" stage which means they must be willing "to create learning environments that incorporate transformation and change into their operating systems" (ibid, 85).

This is the prelude to going public ("activation") with real structural, interactional, and enduring change in relationships. Reconciled groups work together to educate and advocate for others and for their own enduring process of transformation. The lives of the people living through this process of "holistic transformation" are positively affected with not only personal flourishing but a flourishing of their reconciled groups. Through this entire process of growth, the holistic embrace of the others, and solidification of the transformational process, she writes, "we become prophetic witnesses to the reality of the kingdom of God" (ibid, 125), bringing justice, kindness, deep and meaningful relationships, and ultimately greater joy into the world.

5.2. In *Transcending Racial Barriers: Toward a Mutual Obligations Approach,* Michael O. Emerson and George Yancey do not come to the problem of racial conflict in the US from a religious point of view, but rather from a practical and pragmatic point of view. Nevertheless, they describe a process of experiencing the conflict, working to understand the conflict, entering into dialogue with the other to address possible solutions to the conflict, and moving forward into enduring institutionalized solutions in ways that are strikingly similar to those in *Roadmap to Reconciliation*. The dialogue cannot be "accusatory and linear," and it must overcome the "self-interest" of groups that see group selfishness as something positive and necessary (2011, 65, 68). The dialogue must discover a larger "self-interest" or "set of values" that embraces the conflicting parties.

They identify various ways that racial conflict can be addressed, for example, through assimilation, through mutuality, or through multiculturalism. They point out that assimilation is not the best solution: For distinct groups to come together, they must have a core and they must have distinctions." Under the option of "mutuality," people find ways "to remain diverse, with unique cultures, and to share a common core" (2011, 116-17). They point out that the work of sustained examination of the conflict and dialogue directed to reconciling the conflict needs to identify shared interests and shared values that transcend the differences of the groups. In the light of this more embracing shared vision, the differences between the groups become something to be valued and embraced.

For Brenda Salter McNeil these larger values were clearly the commandments of Jesus that we should love one another and live within harmonious communities of respect and concern for one another. Emerson and Yancey suggest "common concerns" and "mutual obligations" as ways to transcend conflict within a larger community of respect and concern. The freedom of all is enhanced, and human flourishing in peace becomes more possible.

5.3. In his book *A Public Peace Process: Sustained Dialogue to Transform Racial and Ethnic Conflicts*, Harold H. Saunders examines citizen initiatives to address conflicts that arise worldwide that the nation-state system does not effectively address. His primary examples of the peace process involve the "inter-Tajik dialogue," the Israeli-Palestinian dialogue, and racial conflict in Baton Rouge, Louisiana. When what is now Tajikistan became independent from the former Soviet Union, the country, made up of multiple ethnic and racial groups, found itself in a violent struggle for unity and a sense of nationhood. Many independent citizens participated in a prolonged process to bring peace to this emergent country. He also describes the process of racial conflict in Baton Rouge in terms of a similar peace process.

The five stage peace process that all these conflicts entered upon, outlined by Saunders, appears strikingly similar to the processes described by the above authors. He remarks that "the idea of a peace process is more important than the details, important as they are" (1999, 29). To deal with racial and ethnic conflict requires that people work together and create a multi-stage process that begins with identifying the problems, getting beyond mutual accusation to a real dialogue concerning the problems and how to move forward, mapping the problem, naming it and framing choices" (ibid., 61), setting a direction, and "acting together" (65). The purpose of this process is to create a larger framework involving mutual understanding that removes misconceptions and embraces a more holistic set of values and interests.

He emphasizes that relationships are extremely important in this process. Institutional change and creating new structures to solidify a larger framework that establishes peace among the parties is not sufficient without developing good person to person and group to group relationships. This idea of changed relationships depends in good measure, all these authors recognize, on the language in which the dialogues are framed and the self-awareness among the participants on how they are using language and framing the issues.

5.4. This issue of language is examined in detail in *Nonviolent Communication: A Language of Life* by Marshall B. Rosenberg.

Perhaps this book should serve as a primer for all those who wish to address racial, ethnic, or any sort of conflict in our lives, from marriage, to family, to working relationships. Rosenberg reviews the forms of speech that block communication. These include "moralistic judgments, making comparisons, denial of responsibility," and a multitude of forms of speech that block relationships or genuine communication (2015, 15-24).

People must learn to "observe without judging" as well as how to identify and express their feelings and needs in such ways that the other can identify with similar feelings and needs in themselves. This opens the way, on both sides, to "the power of empathy" (ibid., 113-128). We begin to deal with our anger and to take responsibility for our anger, seeing it as stemming from our own judgmental process, first and foremost. We must learn to think in terms of our own needs and the needs of others and how these can be expressed as well as addressed through mutual cooperation.

He writes: "It takes tremendous energy and awareness to recognize this destructive learning and to transform it into thoughts and behaviors that are of value and service to life" (ibid., 195). Our cultures worldwide train us to negatively judge others who are different from us. They train us to objectify others in ways that make compassion and empathy difficult or impossible. In this book, Rosenberg holds out a higher value to us in terms of which we can unite: the value of our common humanity, affirming life together, and living together in peace, empathy, and mutual respect. And he makes very clear that the mutual actualization of this higher value requires a sustained process on the part of the participants, whether groups or individuals. In this respect, his book exhibits fundamental agreement with all the above authors.

5.5. Finally, let us consider the book *Making Enemies: Humiliation and International Conflict* by Evelin Lindner.

Throughout her career, Evelin Lindner has studied human social and psychological patterns with a view to understanding how these patterns (from our use of language, to our cultural rituals, to our passive acceptance of structural injustices) continue to humiliate, degrade, and exploit persons around the globe to the advantage of others in a "vertical hierarchy" of implied and assumed worth (2006, 6-10). Men degrade women in these ways, different races degrade one another, tribes (as in Rwanda) degrade other tribes, religions (as in Myanmar) degrade other religions and ethnic groupings. Nationalism, virulent within most countries, degrades people from other countries. All these conflicts can result in horrifying violence, war, and even in genocide.

Evelin Lindner takes her stand on the new paradigm that has emerged primarily in the 20th century and yet has to be assimilated and internalized in our human relationships: the paradigm of human dignity expressed in the 1948 UN Universal Declaration of Human Rights: "All human beings are born free and equal in dignity and rights" (ibid., xiv). The understanding of the meaning of equal dignity for all persons serves as a standard by which we can measure and assess patterns and practices of human humiliation. This book reveals patterns of humiliation and elucidates processes by which we can deal with violations of human dignity (for both groups and persons). The peace process here is quite similar to those processes discussed by the authors considered above.

If it is true that conflicting groups must identify common interests and values that allow them to construct and institutionalize relationships that preserve these larger frameworks, then Lindner is identifying the framework that can unite us all everywhere on this planet:

When asked, "Who are you?" or "Where are you from?" I could reply, "I am a human being from planet Earth, and this is my primary *identity. Apart from that I have a great number of emotional ties to different geographical regions on this planet, to different people from everywhere, and to different occupational, intellectual, and spiritual realms; however, all this is secondary to me being a human being." We need to think in layers of identity, with commonalities forming the highest order of identity, and differences the lowest. Universality can contain diversity, but diversity cannot always contain commonality. World peace requires us to stop giving priority to differences. As long as I believe that my culture is separated from yours by an unbridgeable gulf, we are going to have a problem. Only when I make clear that my being different does not threaten us as human beings who are equal in dignity can I invite you to celebrate our diversity together. (Ibid., 145)*

As a promoter of peace and reconciliation, Linder has been all around the world working with people, such as the survivors of the Rwanda genocide, on healing, reconciliation, and moving forward in peace and justice. Her context for reconciliation is identified here: "I am a human being from planet Earth," just as you are. This is the direction in which healthy human growth points. It involves a continuous self-actualization in truth and love. Ultimately, it embraces us all and lays the foundation for a planet based on peace and justice. We need to start somewhere and that somewhere is here and now.

Conclusion: Overcoming Ethnic, Racial, and Group Conflict

Ethnic, religious, and group conflict is always within a larger context. This context may include a history in which one or more of the parties has experienced trauma at the hands of the other party and continues to live with that trauma. The larger context may also include the common historical roots of the parties, their common language and cultural background. Addressing a conflict requires bringing the larger context to awareness and appealing to it as a framework for interpreting (or perhaps reinterpreting) the relationship and the present conflict.

From the point of view of contemporary scientific holism, the larger context will always include our common humanity and the immense number of linkages that inform the relationship between the conflicting parties. Holism, we have seen, recognizes the unity in diversity of all groups, races, ethnicities, religions, or nations. The whole provides a field of value that is often lacking within the narrow parameters of the conflict but which, once recognized, works to change the conflictual relationships.

From the point of view of mature religion, the whole includes the holism of humanity but goes beyond it to the whole of the divine Ground of Existence. The holism of mature religion needs to bring this larger context into greater awareness. We are all children of God. We all possess Buddha nature. We are all one family as the Upanishads declare: *vasudhaiva kutumbakam.*

These statements are not mere slogans; they are realities that need to be recognized. If we delineate our differences and the roots of our conflict within this larger context, the relationship of conflict itself begins to change, to be interpreted differently. Our devotion to love and truth allows us to interpret the relationship in this larger, more embracing way. In his commentary on the *Bhagavad Gita,* S. Radhakrishnan writes: "By developing our inner spiritual nature, we gain a new kind of relatedness to the world and grow into the freedom, where the integrity of the self is not compromised. We then become aware of ourselves as active creative individuals, not by the discipline of external authority but by the inward rule of free devotion to truth" (1973, 44-45). Clinging to truth (satyagraha) really "shall set us free."

Perhaps the largest practical context that can promote and secure peace is itself the Constitution for the Federation of Earth in which war will be ended, human rights protected equally for all, poverty ultimately eliminated, and a sustainable civilization, based on sound ecological principles, established for the Earth. All these larger contexts, from authentic religion to human rights to Earth Federation make clear that our boundaries and borders are contingent, and therefore our conflicts are also contingent and relative, depending, in part, on how much we emphasize the borders and boundaries at the expense of the larger context.

Ethnic, racial, and group differences are more accidental and less real than the context of unity in diversity that pervades the holism of our human situation. The peace process needs to inform our thinking and our action each day of our lives, for it is also the process of growing in truth and love. The peace process goes to the very heart of genuine religion.

Works Cited

Agnivesh, Swami. 2015. *Applied Spirituality.* New York: Harper-Collins.

Anderson, Benedict. 2006. *Imagined Communities: Reflections on the Origin and Spread of Nationalism.* New York: Verso Press.

Bohm, David. 1980. *Wholeness and the Implicate Order.* New York: Routledge & Kegan Paul.

Boundary-less World: www.boundaryless.net.

Capra, Fitjof. 1996. *The Web of Life: A New Scientific Understanding of Living Systems.* New York: Random House.

De Martino, Richard. 1960. "Zen Buddhism and the Human Situation" in Eric Fromm, D.T. Suzuki, and Richard De Martino, *Psychoanalysis and Zen Buddhism.* New York: Harper & Row, pp. 142-71.

Donnelly, Jack. 2003. *Human Rights in Theory and Practice. Second Edition.* Ithaca: Cornell University Press.

Earth Constitution: www.earth-constitution.org.

Emerson, Michael O. and George Yancey. 2011. *Transcending Racial Barriers: Toward a Mutual Obligations Approach.* Oxford: Oxford University Press.

Ferré, Frederick. 1982. "The Search for a Postmodern Consciousness: The Sense of Mystery," in *The Challenge of Religion: Contemporary Readings in Philosophy of Religion.* Eds. Frederick Ferré, Jospeh J. Kockelmans, John E. Smith. New York: The Seabury Press, pp. 345-51.

Fromm, Erich. 1950. *Psychoanalysis and Religion.* New York: Bantam Books.

Glover. Jonathan. 1999. *Humanity: A Moral History of the 20th Century.* New Haven, CT: Yale University Press.

Happold, F.C. 1966. *Religious Faith & Twentieth-Century Man.* New York: Crossroad Publishers.

Hick, John. 2004. *An Interpretation of Religion: Human Responses to the Transcendent. Second Edition.* New Haven: Yale University Press.

Jesudasan, Ignatius, S.J. 1984. *A Gandhian Theology of Liberation.* Maryknoll, NY: Orbis Books.

Kant, Immanuel. 1964. *Groundwork of the Metaphysic of Morals.* Trans. H. J. Paton. New York: Harper & Row.

Kant, Immanuel. 1983. *Perpetual Peace and Other Essays.* Trans. Ted Humphrey. Indianapolis, IN: Hackett Publishing Company.

Krieger, David J. 1991. *The New Universalism: Foundations for a Global Theology.* Maryknoll, NY: Orbis Books.

Kohlberg, Lawrence. 1984. *The Psychology of Moral Development: Volume Two, The Nature and Validity of Moral Stages.* San Francisco: Harper & Row.

Küng, Hans. 1988. *Theology for the Third Millennium: An Ecumenical View.* Trans. Peter Heinegg. New York: Doubleday Publishers.

Lindner, Evelin. 2006. *Making Enemies: Humiliation and International Conflict.* Westport, CT: Praeger Security International.

Martin, Glen T., ed. 2010. *Constitution for the Federation of Earth: With Historical Introduction, Commentary, and Conclusion.* Appomattox, VA: Institute for Economic Democracy Press.

Martin, Glen T. 2018. *Human Self-Transcendence and Our Global Social Contract: The Power of the Future within Freedom, Dignity, Community, Human Rights, and Global Ethics.* Newcastle upon Tyne, UK: Cambridge Scholars Publishing.

McNeil, Brenda Salter. 2015. *Roadmap to Reconciliation: Moving Communities into Unity, Wholeness, and Justice.* Downers Grove, IL: InterVarsity Press.

O'Brien, Elmer, S.J. 1964. *Varieties of Mystic Experience.* New York: Hold, Rinehart and Winston.

Otto, Rudolf. 1932. *Mysticism East and West: A Comparative Analysis of the Nature of Mysticism.* Trans. Bertha L. Bracey and Richenda C. Payne. New York: The Macmillan Company.

Panikkar, Raimon. 1979. *Myth, Faith, and Hermeneutics: Cross-cultural Studies.* New York: Paulist Press.

Radhakrishnan, S. 1973. *The Bhagavadgita: With an Introductory Essay, Sanskrit Text, English Translation and Notes by S. Radhakrishnan.* New York: Harper Torchbooks.

Rosenberg, Marshall B. 2015. *Nonviolent Communication: A Language of Life.* Encinitas, CA: Puddle Dancer Press.

Saunders, Harold H. 1999. *Public Peace Process: Sustained Dialogue to Transform Racial and Ethnic Conflicts.* New York: Palgrave Publishers.

Schuon, Frithjof. 1975. *The Transcendent Unity of Religions.* Intro. Huston Smith. New York: Harper Torchbooks.

Stace, Walter. 1960. *Mysticism and Philosophy.* London: Macmillan Press.

Tillich, Paul. 1957. *The Dynamics of Faith,* New York: Harper Torchbooks, 1957, 52.

Valadez, Jorge M. 2008. "Adaptation, Sustainability, and Justice," in Randall E. Osborne and Paul Kriese, Eds. *Global Community. Global Security.* Amsterdam, NY: Rodopi Press, pp. 257-74.

COMMUNICATION IN THE DEVELOPMENT OF ETHNIC AND RACIAL CONFLICT
Bruce L. Cook

The Centrality of Communication

Prejudices formed and fostered by verbal and nonverbal communication lead to racial or ethnic conflict.

Communication has served as unwitting cause or willing facilitator of ethnic and racial conflicts over the years. In some cases, it has caused conflict. In other occasions, it has become a tool for oppression. In any case, it has been a necessary component in creation and resolution of these conflicts. Thus, it is hoped that communication may offer a solution for the grave problems ethnic conflicts have caused for humanity.

The present study emphasizes the centrality of communication in human conflict, asserting that ethnic and racial conflict often reflect a human tendency to seek power. While often cloaked as differences in religion or culture, the underlying problems can be traced to a selfish and excessive desire for more of something. Power-seekers use communication to assert themselves and gain selfish ends. In this study, communication is broadly defined as information transfer among human participants, and can even include movement of human participants from one place to another.

Prejudices formed and fostered by verbal and nonverbal communication lead to discrimination which leads to exploitation or even enslavement of one community or race by another, resulting in conflict. The underlying issues are communication which develops and fosters racial and ethnic prejudice.

Origins of Racial and Ethnic Conflict

As a starting point, imagine the earliest moments in human history, a world in time in which populations had not yet experienced any ethnic or racial conflicts. While this early period is impossible to access through direct observation, the literature does offer useful comments.

One source suggests that early caveman communication would have been nonverbal (Kaushal, 2014), while intergroup communication would have been similar to sports teams in today's world:

Through shared experience and belonging, tribal members build their individual identities. Sport offers a tribal arena for collective identification and community expression (Smith & Westerbeek, 2004).

An optimistic researcher might search records of physical anthropology and hope to find evidence that early man existed without ethnic or racial conflicts.

General reports of ancient communities do reveal some interpersonal differences within groups:

...mothers from an interdependent ecosocial context (i.e., rural farmers with low formal schooling from Cameroon or India) regarded the child as an apprentice embedded in a tight social network and showed less face-to-face interaction (Enos, 2011).

Some differences may be ascribed to increases in density of the population. Perhaps ancient humans only began to experience conflicts when there was some crowding or scarcity of desirable land.

...human populations are seen as being in a constant process of adaptation to their natural environment, and which emphasize factors such as economic activity (hunting, gathering, farming, etc.) and population density (Enos, 2011).

Considering an actual report based on physical anthropology, one finds evidence from ancient Oaxaca community life and farming. Notably, there were correlations of social systems with agricultural systems and social/political complexity. Also, there was evidence of ceremonial centers. However, the expectation that early farmers would live in peaceful cooperation is shattered with the finding that at least one set of glyphs carved in stone depicts a battle where neighboring peoples fought, including pictures of slain and mutilated captives (Flannery, Kirkby, Kirkby & Williams, 1967).

A 2002 study concerning Greece in the 1880's, in *Journal of Mediterranean Archaeology* there is mention of slaves in early farming communities (Bintliff, Farinetti, Howard, Sarri & Sbonias, 2002). While it is not possible to ascribe racial or ethnic identity for such slaves, it seems likely that, from early times, some persons have been relegated to inferior status. As mentioned frequently on the PBS program *Finding Your Roots* (Gates, 2018), plantations in Southern US depended on owning slaves to just operate successfully.

From this point it becomes impossible to ignore the fact that persons with power exploited weaker peoples on early contact and enslaved them or otherwise took advantage. For example, in the arrival of early explorers in the Kikuyu area of Eastern Africa, we find this account:

Evidence presented suggests that Kikuyu were initially hospitable to coastal traders. By the 1800's, however, Kikuyu were reluctant to allow free passage of Arab and Swahili caravans. Hostility had been engendered by Arab and Swahili propensities for raiding Kikuyu mashamba for food and departing the area without making restitution. European attitudes toward the Kikuyu were influenced by rumors of Kikuyu ferocity deliberately spread by coastal and Wakamba traders. Early explorers were prepared to "fight every inch of the way" across the Kikuyu habitat. European apprehension coupled with Kikuyu suspicion featured prominently in the early contact period (Toulson, 1976).

Such experiences were common across the diaspora, and this establishes that conflict between long-established communities and those who would exploit their resources was widespread. It is this heinous application of power which constitutes the origin of ethnic and racial conflict, and it could only happen through communication.

Early communication started with language learning (Riley, 1971). Soon the explorers seek resources and, in some cases, try to influence religious belief and otherwise bring Western "civilization" to traditional people. Further, the countries who were preparing to dominate these peoples began to compete to secure the most value for their benefit. (Compare this with the Oaxaca glyths, which revealed that early humans fought to secure and defend adjacent territories. Even there the spirit of cooperation seemed absent.)

Colonization

Thus, communication became a tool in the subjugation of traditional people. The story of colonization is too massive to summarize here, but it becomes important to recognize that communication was the tool that permitted exploitation and competition.

As part of colonization, it was necessary for dominating countries to communicate and trade with their colonies, and this led to many achievements in communication which are now taken for granted (Hornik, 1993). While ships and explorers made the first contacts, it soon became essential for these countries to replace traditional cultures they did not understand with what they saw as essential features of civilization: roads (Rodney, 1972), telegraph lines (Hochschild,1999), and railroads (Monson, 2009).

Underlying the economic and resource dimensions, ethnic bias threatened the weak. Occasionally a leadership technique went far beyond railroads and telegraph lines when it came to establishing lines of power and authority. An often-overlooked technique used by leaders was based on the ancient strategy (Chopra, 2002) – divide and conquer (Belkin, 2012). In this strategy, as often seen in religion today, leaders deliberately turn population subgroups against each other to enhance their control. This has never been more blatant that the situation in Rwanda and Uganda, where colonial leaders divided traditional populations into arbitrary divisions – in this case tall people vs short people (Prunier, 2008). As a point of further shame for the leaders, as reported by Claude Shema Rutagengwa, a chilling situation existed as hate media RTLM Radio 'death media' prepared minds for genocide (Onguny, 2018) by motivating the Hutu majority group to kill the taller Tutsi minority members and their supporters (Shema, 2018). Note again the use of communication to achieve purposes of leaders.

Genocide and the Second World War

Sadly, equally grotesque ethnic and racial conflicts followed. Early exploitation of populations gave way to systematic genocide in a barbaric form of communication in Europe – extermination of six million individuals due to their religion. However, while formerly exploited populations were poor, self-sufficient and traditional, in this case the people to be exterminated were so highly talented and successful that Adolf Hitler and his henchmen feared them and resented their success in Germany's Second Reich (Schleunes, 1990).

Communication was a tool in Hitler's attempts to achieve what he saw as the Final Solution to what he described as the "problem" of the Jews. His insistence on controlling communication and operating in secret was a precursor of today's frequent government actions to control and suppress mass and social media. For example, his technicians developed the Enigma encryption system which made it possible for German forces to communicate across great distances without being understood by enemy forces. His control of mass communication and propaganda was absolute (O'Shaughnessy, 2009).

From a technological point of view, Hitler's European War accelerated technological developments in communication technology. Especially interesting for the present analysis is the fact that three communication developments have been credited with winning a war that was close to victory by Hitler's evil forces:

1) The Polish mathematician Marian Rayewski and others successfully broke the Enigma code (Rejewski, 1981) using the supercomputer Colossus (Copeland, 2010).

2) Developments in radar technology, led by Alfred Loomis and Sir Henry Tizard's British mission to the United States, created a joint venture by British and American scientists to miniaturize and adapt radio frequency radiation so the Allies

could accurately target enemy aircraft (Van Keuren, 1997).

3) Thankfully the German high command failed to accept computing technology proposed to them by Konrad Zuse in 1940, a technological innovation that would have made it possible to accurately aim V2 bombs and accomplish Hitler's desire of annihilating the city of London (Rojas, 2014).

Solutions

After ethnic monstrosities of the type perpetuated by Hitler, communication became a key element in attempting to reduce ethnic and racial tensions. After the military victory, the Marshall Plan (one of the greatest economic policy and foreign policy successes of this century) (De Long & Eichengreen, 1991), supplemented the development of formal international communication through the United Nations, preceded by the League of Nations (Goodrich,1947), UNESCO (Petitjean, 2007), and the United Nations (Hilderbrand, 2001). These organizations took the lead in restoring peace and attempting to prevent future warfare on a global scale.

At the same time, communication had a vital role in decolonialization. Stevenson's 1988 book, *Communication Development and the Third World,* summarizes these events:

In 1964 Wilbur Schramm, on a grant from the United Nations Educational, Scientific and Cultural Organization (UNESCO), wrote a book called "Mass Media and National Development." It painted a glowing picture in which the mass media would reveal the way to development and enable the Third World countries to achieve in a few decades the development that had occurred over centuries in the West. By the 1970s it became clear that population growth was overtaking development. The Third World nations began to see the mass media as tools of the conspiracy of transnational corporations in their [effort] to keep the Third World a source of cheap labor. The Third World countries began to seek an alternate route to development, without help from either the East or the West. Their ideal and model was China, where the radical alternative had been shown to work. The Third [World] countries joined together as the "Non-Aligned Movement," an organization which had been founded in Indonesia in 1955. By the 1970s the Third World countries constituted a majority in UNESCO, which they turned into a forum of resentment against the Western mass media, which they perceived as using dominance over world news flow to keep the Third World in a state of cultural dependency on the West. The poverty of the Third World nations, they claimed, was the heritage of colonialism, and the West owed them restitution. The Western news media were identified as the modern-day equivalent of the colonial armies of imperialism. The debate over the dominance of Western influence in world news flow was launched in UNESCO by a request from the Soviet Union in 1972 for "a declaration on the fundamental principles governing the use of the mass media with a view to strengthening peace and understanding and combating war, propaganda, radicalism, and apartheid." The debate in UNESCO took on a new name, the "New World Information Order," in which the Third World nations argued that they had the right to restrict the free flow of news across their borders. UNESCO Director General, Amadou M 'Bow, tabled the resolution and appointed a commission, headed by Sean MacBride, to undertake general review of communications problems in modern society. The report, entitled "Many Voices, One World," was in many ways vague, but it at least endorsed the Western values of free flow of information. The US offered technological assistance to the Third World under the auspices of the International Program for the Development of Communication. This institution was designed as a world clearinghouse for communication development, but as such it accomplished little. Meanwhile, the Third World countries gave priority to developing their own national news agencies and the Non-Aligned News Agencies Pool, dedicated to the "journalism of national development." What this meant, in effect, was journalism limited to "development news" (which by definition was always good) and to "protocol news," i.e., ribbon-cutting and other ceremonial events. By the time of the US withdrawal from UNESCO at the end of 1984, the issue was becoming, if not resolved, at least quiescent, with some indications of progress. At the 1983 conference at Talloires, the World Press Freedom Committee and the Associated Press put together a list of 300 journalistic exchange, training, and internship programs in 70 countries. The World Bank issued a report on "Telecommunications and Economic Development," and a report by the Organization for Economic Cooperation and Development and the International Telecommunications Union pointed out the cost-benefit relationship of telecommunications to economic development. Finally, a report by an international commission headed by Sir Donald Maitland stressed the importance of shifting existing resources to telecommunications so that basic communications services would be available to everyone on earth by the early 21st century (Stevenson, 1988).

The period of formal colonization did end (Pearce, 2005) and it is important to recognize that communication had been an active participant in the solutions. As an important caveat, the termination of colonialism left many traces of neo-colonialism and imperialism (Nkrumah, 1966). The history of colonization of Africa by alien peoples has been chronicled by Johnston (2011), who concluded that "the eventual outcome of the colonization of Africa by alien races [would] be a compromise" of races. The colonial state basically decayed into crisis by the 1980s with external and internal pressures. At the same time, the continent endured an erosion of many African polities by the 1990s, which limited reform and provoked a complex web of civil conflicts (Young, 2004). Even now it's important to review the crises that beset the African continent and evaluate the checkered record of European colonial rule in Africa (Babou, 2010).

The stage was set for an idyllic period of peace after the Second World War and formal colonization. However, the desired consensus quickly became a myth (Owen, 1996). Instead, these major nightmares were followed by Cold War and Imperialism.

Fortunately for the cause of peace and open communication, Mikhail Gorbachev emerged as the leader of the USSR in 1985 and ended the USSR's tight control of communication with a new age of transparency and openness called "glasnost" (Beschloss & Talbott, 2016). Ultimately the use of power and high-level diplomacy in the conflict unified Germany and brought Europe together along with the 1989 destruction of the Berlin Wall (Ratnesar, 2009), which brought the conflict to an end (Zelikow & Rice,1995). Still, by 1990 it became clear that the unstable situation would not last (Mearsheimer, 1990).

One glaring remnant of colonial control was the continuing apartheid situation in South Africa, where the government deliberately kept its black population in poverty and secondary status to protect the white settlers who had developed many business interests (Thörn, 2006). While this problem of transition from settlers to relative freedom was typical of other areas such as Zambia, the presence of apartheid in South Africa became a rallying call for condemnation by world media in the transnational anti-apartheid movement. Here was a glowing triumph for media in bringing an elitist government to its knees.

The apartheid system in South Africa was ended through a series of negotiations between 1990 and 1993 and through unilateral steps by the de Klerk government. These negotiations took place between the governing National Party, the African National Congress, and a wide variety of other political organizations (Wikipedia, 2018).

The same power of curing colonialism was evident in Sudan, when efforts of African Union (following the Organization of African Unity) aggressively pursued peace in Burundi, Sudan (Sudan, 2000), the Comoros, and Somalia, while addressing similar inequities in many African countries. Here was an achievement in negotiating peace on the African continent, and international media played a secondary role. However, it is possible to believe that international news coverage of their pitiful massacres motivated the Sudan government to accept a split between North and South Sudan. Sadly, the resulting peace has proven temporary, but unexpected hope has arisen now that China has led an initiative to mediate the current conflicts in an effort to protect its interests in the region (Large, 2018).

The year 1999, five years after the Rwandan genocide as well as five years after the liberation of South Africa from the yoke of apartheid, saw the OAU reaching its stated aim to liberate the African continent from colonialism. In this year, African leaders met in Sirte, Libya, to review the OAU Charter. This meeting emphasised the importance of strengthening solidarity among African countries and reviving the spirit of PanAfricanism, borrowed from the ideas of thinkers such as W E B du Bois, Marcus Garvey, Frantz Fanon, Kwame Nkrumah and Léopold Senghor. Faced with mounting problems and the challenges of living in a globalised world there was a movement among African leaders to forge even closer unity on the continent and adopt a project of regional integration. The AU project was born in Sirte in 1999 with the decision to draft an act of constitution. The AU's Constitutive Act was subsequently signed in Lomé, Togo on 11 July 2000. The official inauguration of the AU took place in July 2002 in Durban, South Africa and represented the next level in the evolution of the ideal of Pan-Africanism (Murithi, 2008).

Media and Peace

Once Eastern and Western media were on somewhat the same page, and once everyday people could hope for peace, new developments in communication unalterably changed the situation. In the period 1997-2005, everyday people suddenly achieved access to mass communication via social media. This gave them the information power which had always resided in the networks and newspapers.

Until the age of the Internet, individuals were unable to publish their writings on mass communication systems. Sixdegrees.com started the social media stage in 1997 (Ellison, 2007) and another change occurred when it became possible for individuals to "post" their writings for free on the writing display site, author-me.com (Cook, 2017). This occurred in the early history of many social media networks, such as Facebook.com, MySpace.com and Twitter (Ellison, 2007).

> *"...a fundamental shift of power." It's a shift from pontification to two-way communication.... No longer does the consumer trust our corporate messages.... They want their information from people they know, have a relationship with, and trust. They want to be educated by, hear their news from, and get their product reviews from people they know and trust. They want to share their experiences, both good and bad, with people who trust them (Safko, 2012).*

Innocuous at first, social media eventually became competitive with public networks like the BBC and CBS, etc., to display positive or negative messages and quickly recruit followers. Where membership in political groups used to required physical proximity of subjects or mailed correspondence, it was now possible for individuals to become members of a group on one day and become loyal to another cause or lose interest soon after.

Naturally, the ability of citizens to freely access public media became a threat for autocratic leaders, who frequently have felt fear of social media.

> *Perhaps the most classic example was in Iran, where, starting in 2012 with the election of Iranian President Hasan Rouhani, social media were banned. Only Rouhani could use the medium, hoping to control propaganda from his central government. Much to Rouhani's consternation, university students and others managed to use virtual*

private networks and successfully bypass the state's Internet filtering. Iran's "Ministry of Sciences has reported that 60 percent of Iranian university students use Viber and WeChat, and in a survey of 2,300 people, 58 percent reported using Facebook regularly, and 37 percent said they used Google+ (Etehad, 2014).

Perhaps as a reaction to this type of fear, and in a turn-about-face, US President Donald Trump has resorted to his own personal Twitter account to report news of his administration to millions of citizens (Galdieri, Lucas & Sisco, 2018).

Communication as a Solution

Communication has acted as a tool to create and solve racial and ethnic problems throughout history. Considering this record, it's worthwhile to evaluate communication solutions which might reduce racial and ethnic conflicts in the future. As a caveat, though, please recognize the possibility that other solutions would be more effective, such as giving international leadership powers to women primarily, with participation of men at the level currently assigned to women. For women, the author believes, would make decisions about conflicts with a presence of compassion that seems absent today. Additionally, their decisions would show new respect for future implications of current events.

First, when it comes to applications of communication in racial and ethnic conflicts, it's important to recognize that these conflicts – while very real – are usually an offshoot of human failings. Typically, they do not relate directly to the content or dogma or beliefs of any particular racial or ethnic group. As a classic example, consider that Hitler did not kill six million Jewish people because he objected to their religious practices or beliefs. In fact, he envied and feared the talents and skills of this group, which was having such success in German culture, business and government, and so he decided to kill them so he and his fellow

Aryan Germans could possess unchallenged power (Schleunes, 1990). The problem was not race, ethnicity, or religion – the problem was power.

Similarly, in other racial and ethnic conflicts presented above, power is usually the problem, and communication lends itself well to greedy purposes of persons and groups which are obsessed with increasing their power. As seen in the chronicle of time, the quest for more power, more money, and absolute control can lead to incredible brutality. It is a problem of extremes (McClelland, 1970). Think of a King (even in the modern age) and how he continues to encourage his followers to kill thousands of individuals just to enhance his personal power and glory. Across history, such behavior is not unusual. However, it is high time to stop it, for the advent of nuclear power has made it possible for an autocratic leader to destroy the world.

Can communication limit such irrational quests for power? As seen in the analysis above, it is possible for communication to influence such leaders to become more responsible. As an example, witness the power of international condemnation when the governments of South Africa and Sudan were continuing their oppression of black persons.

More than in theory, international communication can bring to the public, international shame to the power-obsessed leaders. While this could theoretically be accomplished by an international agency like the United Nations, the sad truth has been that such agencies themselves become vulnerable to contamination by power-obsessed nations, thus rendering the agencies ineffective. Even an international court risks control by power-obsessed leaders and participants.

As an alternative, it is suggested that international news media take the lead in saving the world from power-obsessed individuals and groups. This would fly in the face of advocacy journalism and require a major reduction in the movement to advocacy journalism, where journalists themselves, like politicians, become even more engaged in power brokering (Davis, 2003). As an urgent alternative, it is suggested that international journalists establish an independent group to meet and consider the relative importance of using their power to save the world from nuclear devastation. This, of course, would oppose the host of today's journalists who seem intent on exposing news without regard to any damaging effects on society, thus winning readers and viewers for the benefit of their own reputations and those of their organizations.

Supporting this idea, it's worthwhile to recognize the increasing efforts of news organization in presenting good news spin as part of their content, such as that of David Muir of ABC News with his *America Strong* stories (Muir, 2017).

This call for a new responsibility implores journalists to act independently of their political and management associates. With strong self-regulation, they can set standards for screening their stories to prevent information from exposure if it will have damaging effects on society. For example, they would be expected to block a story which instructed readers and viewers on how to construct a bomb. Or, perhaps, they would choose not to endlessly report a story on drive-by shootings or killings in a public school.

There is a need for journalists to create a new connotation for evils in racial and ethnic conflicts, and also for the problem of nuclear weapons. A recent publication on minimizing the danger of nuclear weapons has suggested that limiting or controlling the number of nuclear bombs will not prove feasible as a practical matter, for, after denuclearization, one or another country will always be able to secretly restart the nuclear threat. As a practical alternative, that study calls for giving the nuclear conflict the same negative connotation as cannibalism, so that anyone in the world, including power-obsessed leaders, will want nothing to do with using nuclear weapons.

For example, my abhorrence at eating human flesh is likely to ensure that I do not do so, whether or not I believe others share this abhorrence. But in the case of nuclear weapons, unless I believe that my abhorrence is shared by the leaders of other states, it is much less likely that my abhorrence will insure that I do not use the weapons. In addition, the use of nuclear weapons might occur as the result of a sort of blind escalatory process, in which my attitudes may not be fully in control of my actions. But there is no analogous process regarding the abhorrence of cannibalism or other sorts of delegitimized behavior. So, the negative attitudes in the case of nuclear weapons use must be much stronger to insure nonuse than is the case with behaviors such as cannibalism (Lee, 2018).

Applying this to the problem of racial and ethnic conflicts, journalists can foster public revulsion over power plays of leaders and nations that create disgusting racial and ethnic conflicts. Hopefully this can save the world from mankind's continuing record of oppressing and murdering in a greedy quest to control more resources than others. Here is a devastating situation well worth solving. If communication is to have a role, it is highly recommended that a self-regulating group of independent journalists step up to the challenge.

References

Babou, C. A. (2010). Decolonization or National liberation: debating the end of British Colonial Rule in Africa. *The ANNALS of the American Academy of Political and Social Science*, 632(1), 41-54.

Belkin, A. (2012). *United we stand?: divide-and-conquer politics and the logic of international hostility.* SUNY Press.

Beschloss, M., & Talbott, S. (2016). *At the highest levels: The inside story of the end of the Cold War.* Open Road Media.

Bintliff, J., Farinetti, E., Howard, P., Sarri, K., & Sbonias, K. (2002). Classical farms, hidden prehistoric landscapes and

Greek rural survey: a response and an update. *Journal of Mediterranean Archaeology,* 15(2), p. 262.

Chopra, D. (2002). *The soul of leadership.* School Administrator, 59(8), 10-13.

Cook, B.L., (2017). Voice of social media: 1999-2017, Adacemia.edu, 2017. Retrieved from https://www.academia.edu/34567275/Voice_of_Social_media_1999-2017.docx

Copeland, B. J. (Ed.). (2010). *Colossus: The secrets of Bletchley Park's code-breaking computers.* Oxford University Press.

Davis, A. (2003). Whither mass media and power? Evidence for a critical elite theory alternative. *Media, Culture & Society,* 25(5), 669-690.

De Long, J. B., & Eichengreen, B. (1991). The Marshall Plan: History's most successful structural adjustment program (No. w3899). *National Bureau of Economic Research.*

Ellison, N. B. (2007). Social network sites: Definition, history, and scholarship. *Journal of Computer-Mediated Communication,* 13(1), 210-230.

Enos, T. (Ed.). (2011). *Encyclopedia of rhetoric and composition: Communication from ancient times to the information age.* Routledge, p. 51.

Etehad, M. Why are Twitter and Facebook still blocked in Iran?, Aljazeera (April 19, 2014). Retrieved from http://america.aljazeera.com/opinions/2014/4/iran-twitter-rouhaniinternetcensorship.html

Flannery, K. V., Kirkby, A. V., Kirkby, M. J., & Williams, A. W. (1967). Farming systems and political growth in ancient Oaxaca. *Science,* 158(3800), 445-454.

Galdieri, C. J., Lucas, J. C., & Sisco, T. S. (2018). Introduction: Politics in 140 Characters or Less. In *The Role of Twitter in the 2016 US Election* (pp. 1-5). Palgrave Pivot, Cham.

Gates, H. L. (2018). *Finding Your Roots,* 2018. Retrieved from http://www.pbs.org/weta/finding-your-roots/home.

Goodrich, L. M. (1947). *From League of Nations to United Nations.* International Organization, 1(1), 3-21.

Hilderbrand, R. C. (2001). *Dumbarton Oaks: the origins of the*

United Nations and the search for postwar security. UNC Press Books.

Hochschild, A. (1999). *King Leopold's ghost: A story of greed, terror, and heroism in colonial Africa.* Houghton Mifflin Harcourt. P. 27.

Hornik, R. C. (1993). *Development communication: Information, agriculture, and nutrition in the Third World.* University Press of America.

Johnston, H. H. (2011). *A history of the colonization of Africa by alien races.* Cambridge University Press.

Kaushal, S. (2014). Different aspects of intercultural nonverbal communication: a study. *Asian J. of Adv. Basic Sci,* 2(2), p. 31.

Large, D. (2018). Sudan and South Sudan: A Testing Ground for Beijing's Peace and Security Engagement. In *China and Africa* (pp. 163-178). Palgrave Macmillan, Cham.

Lee, S.P. (2018). Minimizing the Danger of Nuclear Weapons. In *Handbook of Research on Examining Global Peacemaking in the Digital Age* (pp. 45-50). IGI Global, p. 49.

McClelland, D. C. (1970). The two faces of power. *Journal of international Affairs,* 29-47.

Mearsheimer, J. J. (1990). Back to the future: Instability in Europe after the Cold War. *International security,* 15(1), 5-56.

Monson, J. (2009). *Africa's Freedom Railway: how a Chinese development project changed lives and livelihoods in Tanzania.* Indiana University Press.

Muir, D. World News Tonight – America Strong, ABC News, 2017. Retrieved from http://abcnews.go.com/WNT/fullpage/david-muir-world-news-tonights-america-strong-39653377

Murithi, T. (2008). The African Union's evolving role in peace operations: the African Union Mission in Burundi, the African Union Mission in Sudan and the AfricanUnion Mission in Somalia. *African Security Studies,* 17(1), 69-82, p. 73.

Nkrumah, K. (1966). *Neo-Colonialism: The Last Stage of Imperialism.* 1965. New York: International.

Toulson, T. (1976). *Europeans and the Kikuyu to 1910: a study of resistance, collaboration and conquest* (Doctoral dissertation,

University of British Columbia).

O'Shaughnessy, N. (2009). Selling Hitler: propaganda and the Nazi brand. *Journal of Public Affairs*, 9(1), 55-76.

Onguny, P. (2018). International news coverage of insecurity and human suffering in Africa's great lakes region. *Journal of Media Critiques* [JMC], 3(12), p. 126.

Owen, N. (1996). *Decolonisation and postwar consensus. In The Myth of Consensus* (pp. 157-181). Palgrave Macmillan, London.

Pearce, R. D. (2005). *The turning point in Africa: British Colonial policy 1938-48.* Routledge.

Petitjean, P. (2007, September). The" Periphery Principle": Unesco and the international commitment of scientists after World War II. In *The 'Periphery Principle': UNESCO and the international commitment of scientists after World War II* (pp. 734-741). *Cracow: The Polish Academy of Arts and Sciences.*

Prunier, G. (2008). *Africa's world war: Congo, the Rwandan genocide, and the making of a continental catastrophe.* Oxford University Press.

Ratnesar, R. (2009). *Tear Down This Wall: A City, a President, and the Speech that Ended the Cold War.* Simon and Schuster.

Rejewski, M. (1981). How Polish mathematicians broke the Enigma cipher. *Annals of the History of Computing,* 3(3), 213-234.

Riley, C. L. (1971). Early Spanish-Indian communication in the greater Southwest. *New Mexico Historical Review,* 46(4), 285.

Rodney, W. (1972). How Europe underdeveloped Africa. *Beyond borders: Thinking critically about global issues,* p. 108.

Rojas, R. (2014). Konrad Zuse's Proposal for a Cipher Machine. Cryptologia, 38(4), 362-369.

Safko, L. (2012). *The Social Media Bible.* John Wiley & Sons, Inc., 2012, p. 3.

Schleunes, K. A. (1990). *The twisted road to Auschwitz: Nazi policy toward German Jews,* 1933-1939. University of Illinois Press, pp. 4-5.

Shema, C. R. (2018). Peacebuilding, Media and Terrorism in 21st Century and Beyond: A Psychological Perspective.

In *Handbook of Research on Examining Global Peacemaking in the Digital Age* (pp. 224-242). IGI Global, p. 232.

Smith, A., & Westerbeek, H. (2004). *Caveman, fan and clan. In The Sport Business Future* (p. 74). Palgrave Macmillan UK.

Stevenson, R. L. (1988). Communication development and the Third World. *The global politics of information.*

Sudan, C. D. I. (2000). Brave new century. *Africa Confidential*, 41(1).

Thörn, H. (2006). *Anti-apartheid and the emergence of a global civil society.* Springer.

Van Keuren, D. K. (1997). Science goes to war: The radiation laboratory, radar, and their technological consequences. *Reviews in American History*, 25(4), 643-647.

Wikipedia, Negotiations to end apartheid in South Africa, Retrieved from https://en.wikipedia.org/wiki/Negotiations_to_end_apartheid_in_South_Africa

Young, C. (2004). The end of the post-colonial state in Africa? Reflections on changing African political dynamics. *African Affairs*, 103(410), 23-49.

Zelikow, P., & Rice, C. (1995). *Germany unified and Europe transformed: a study in statecraft* (Vol. 528). Cambridge, MA: Harvard University Press.

RESOLVING OUTER CULTURAL CONFLICTS BY GOING WITHIN
Harold W. Becker

A Different Perspective

From this core sense of inner awareness of our truth, versus what we accepted from others, we can unravel and transform long-held belief patterns that no longer serve.

For countless millennia and for reasons we rarely question or comprehend, our various cultures and traditions continue to teach us to be wary of strangers and anyone unfamiliar or different in some way to us. This fundamental flaw in our individual and collective understanding, where we see others as dissimilar, weaker, or as a threat, leads to successive generations of ongoing discrimination with cycles of violence, suffering, war, and needless death. We continue to invoke these behaviors as a reaction to our mistaken perspective that we are somehow separate from each other, rather than recognizing our common human heritage. Let us seek to finally overcome this inertia and begin to view the value of diversity in our world with wisdom, compassion, kindness, and love.

There are innumerable reasons and justifications on how we came to believe we are somehow separate from each other and ourselves. Whether initially well intentioned efforts to protect family, community and resources, for example, to simply coming to identify with sameness of our surroundings and experiences - being uncomfortable with anything that is contrary to our perception of a status quo became threatening. In response, we exacerbated these conditions by further withdrawing into our singular worlds by creating walls, boundaries, borders and corresponding traditions – figuratively and literally. Racial and ethnic divides are one example of our unwitting and misguided approach to our human neighbors.

At what point do we determine a stranger became our friend? How would life be different if our perspective naturally embraced each fellow human as a friend first? These may sound like broad philosophical questions, yet they underscore and reveal our present personal life view. Our answers also indicate our current relationship with other humans, and perhaps more importantly, how we perceive ourselves. When we fully comprehend that the spark of life that beats our heart is the same in everyone else, we embark on a journey where we know that we make a powerful, positive difference with each thought, feeling, word, deed and action.

By going within and asking ourselves essential questions as to who we truly are, and our universal connection to one another, we reconnect to our heart center. From this core sense of inner awareness of our truth, versus what we accepted from others, we start to unravel and transform long-held belief patterns that no longer serve. This personal choice to go within and determine our sense of self is a crucial step towards a sustainable and peaceful planet where our cultures and traditions thrive together as one.

Realizing that we, collectively and historically, base most of our interactions with one another from ideas of separation, limitation, fear and ignorance helps us also find the causal component that can resolve these same issues. Racial and ethnic conflicts are one of the outer expression examples that finds its roots in a myriad of distorted perspectives about life. By focusing on appearances and basing assumptions from learned and accepted false notions handed down by others, we place judgment upon those around us in an attempt to strengthen our own worldview. If there is a challenge in response, we often become verbally shaming and abusive and eventually physically violent towards others in an attempt to force and maintain our perspective.

Do we see ourselves as weak and helpless, different and singular, or possibly superior and dominating? Each of these perspectives provides insights to our individual and cultural ingrained beliefs, views, assumptions and opinions. Passed from generation to generation without question, by family, teachers, leaders, experiences and circumstances, and even at times, by our environmental conditions, we perpetuate our stories of insecurity, disconnect, judgment, indignity and humiliation. There is another story to tell and that is the one where we become the aware, compassionate and empowered collective that changes the paradigm. Beginning within, this new story acknowledges the value of every life form.

By reuniting with our personal heart-centered wisdom, we restore our conscious choice with each intention and interaction with the world around us. We become the catalyst for change in our families, communities, cultures and traditions. Thankfully, this essential change is already happening and through us, our collective perspective will expand far beyond the current conditions and lead to some truly astounding revelations, opportunities and unfathomable potentials.

An Awakening World

An unfolding journey of awakening and self-discovery is underway around the globe and it is revealing a vast new awareness that is far beyond the scope of prescribed education, leadership, traditions and cultural norms that we are accustomed to participating in. With the unfolding real-time social interactions brought about by the worldwide web, our access to one another is becoming instant, cross cultural and directly personal. These new forms of communication with one another are initiating a process where we are questioning the many different concepts and suggestions shared through longstanding information channels. It is becoming more evident with each passing moment that most are an attempt at conformity and compliance to social and behavioral standards of the past that are rapidly becoming outdated and outmoded.

We often disguise our personal doubts, challenges, fears, and emotions, for instance, under the pretense of appropriate and acceptable behavior as part of our life view, teachings and opinions. We do this in an endeavor to ensure a more stable social outer order and maintain a standard on individual and group beliefs. Yet, the primary challenge remains; we consider anyone outside these imposed social structures to be a stranger or a threat, and this perspective instantly creates separation. Separation is the pain we all suffer from and it is really an illusion. We are all interconnected and interdependent on this beautiful blue orb we call earth.

When we return to the bigger picture of life, we instantly connect to the deepest aspect of our kindred being. This connection sees the oneness in each other and, from this angle, only kindness prevails and diversity is expected and celebrated. Kindness certainly knows no borders and flows with ease and grace when we allow it to express itself through us. Diversity allows us to share these many experiences in a variety of ways that enhance our journey of life.

Moving beyond our limiting beliefs and choosing to see everyone as a friend, opens us up to a global diversity beyond comprehension. By trusting ourselves, we become more intimate, natural and embracing with each person we encounter in life. When we choose to see life from the viewpoint of unity, our cultures, rituals, customs and social perceptions give way to soul expressions as we allow our heart to guide our destiny. This quiet voice of inner wisdom understands the connection that is ever-present and seeks to encourage us to remember our universal heartbeat. When we approach each other as a friend, we set the stage for grand potential. The word "stranger" ceases to exist in this context and disappears from our vocabulary completely.

Embracing Change

An extraordinary change in consciousness comes with an inherent amount of disorder and confusion as we commence to alter our underlying awareness, intentions, and desires, from pure survival to a more universal and sustainable approach to life. In present times, it often appears to be only chaotic change since our conditioned and polarized stories of fear and lack, judgment, blame, indifference and apathy, have been in place and reinforced for eons. This is all starting to move and open up to greater mindfulness as we realize the possibilities within each of us. When we open our hearts, the beauty of love is obvious and, together, we amplify the profound energy that heals and restores the good in life.

Change requires us to release the old and embrace our potential for something new. During this quantum shift of consciousness, it may initially seem that there is little sense or hope of peace around our world today. Yet, when we look just beyond the appearances, we can see a much greater opportunity unfolding among women's groups, youth groups, the sciences and faith-based organizations, for illustration. Numerous individuals may continue to act from a place of fear and doubt, which includes greed, lust, guilt, anger, self-righteousness and a variety of other lower ego-based actions. However, many more are engaging in peaceful, loving and compassionate responses. Most will not necessarily read about these heart-based individuals in newspapers or see them on television; rather, they will encounter them in their daily journey. These are the everyday citizens who choose love and peace as their way of life in every thought, feeling, word, deed and action.

Love and peace are qualities we cultivate through the conscious choices we make each moment. In this vigorously evolving social information age, it is becoming increasingly important to be aware of our personal thoughts and feelings and discern our truth for ourselves. The choices we make are of our own accord and equally, our chance to share our loving energy from within as a conscious act of self-responsibility. No one can do it for us. By keeping our attention upon the images we desire in our heart, rather than the response or suggestions from outside influences or past memories, we form a more peaceful and prosperous future. Love and peace are growing on the planet and we must first align with a loving and peaceful attitude within to then notice it around us. Embodying these qualities on a personal level provides the means to assist others to become aware of it through our serene expression of this energy.

The Power and Potential of Unconditional Love

For many, the awareness of love is emotional and physical. We frequently ascribe universal or unconditional love to saintly, mystical ideals and unreachable heights compared to our everyday awareness. Perhaps it is time to evolve our understanding and provide a pragmatic definition that assists us in our recognition of this innate potential for each of us. For a closer understanding and useful explanation, we will look at the two words: unconditional and love.

To understand love, we are using more than a descriptive word to characterize our experience of life. Love is energy. It is a power that permeates the universe and at times, we glimpse its infinite nature through experiences in our world. Love is a process and way of living life and is an expansion of certain qualities we can feel physically, emotionally, mentally, and spiritually. It is a sense of personal peace and joy, as well as, an expression of kindness, compassion, and understanding. When we comfort and support ourselves, and those around us, we are tapping into love. To engage the use of love is to forgive and release the appearances of our experiences. Love trusts, is patient and never wishes to judge or hate.

When we love, we are not in fear or doubt. Likewise, we accept responsibility for our actions and do not blame, shame, use aggression, control or manipulate another. Love is freedom from the limiting beliefs that encourage our inner criticism, condemnation, prejudice, anger, hatred and frustration. Love allows lack and limitation, guilt and worry to transform into higher expressions of dreams and possibilities. The simple stillness of love releases worries and concerns, providing new opportunities to experience our lives in joyous ways.

Love is an attitude we have about life and is a thought and feeling we hold within. When we love, we are allowing the highest level of our awareness to permeate the experience of the moment. We are literally vibrating to a higher frequency of energy and allowing that energy to move forth into our world, where it changes and lifts everything it contacts. It is an ever-evolving journey. When we consider all of the qualities that love represents, we realize that love is truly a way of being.

Now that we have defined various aspects of love, let us turn to our other word, unconditional. To be unconditional, is to be without condition - or limit. To be unconditional is to be unlimited. This means no strings attached, no stipulations, and no expectations.

Bringing these two words together form a simple and useful definition: unconditional love is an unlimited way of being. When we approach life without any limit to our thoughts and feelings, and choose to share the many qualities of love each moment, we create realities previously undreamed of as we explore our unlimited imagination. Being fully aware in the present moment, there are infinite imaginative possibilities when we allow the freedom to go beyond our perceived limits. If we can dream it, we can manifest it. With unconditional love as our guiding intention, life becomes a wondrous adventure that excites the very core of our being and lights our path with delight.

For eons, we have accepted the artificial perspective of separation from our true selves and the world around us. This has been the basis for frequent control, domination and enslavement of minds, bodies, societies and cultures, along with countless battles, wars, needless deaths and destruction. While repeatedly ignoring our heart, which knows its innate connection to life, we forge forward with a limited, mental approach to life. The universal wisdom of the heart has been usually misunderstood, mistrusted, and thus regularly suppressed by the incomplete knowledge of the mind. This disconnect born of the separation of the mind and heart led to doubt, which became the experience of fear in its various manifestations that surround us today.

Interestingly, our present day out-of-balance concept of separation has become so obvious that it is creating the inspiration of inquiry that is leading us back to unity and oneness. The disparity and ensuing despair from the innumerable maladies, injustices, irrational judgments and imbalanced material pursuits are arousing our attention to the imperative need to seek greater wisdom in our individual and combined choices.

When we know our connection to all that is, we no longer doubt or fear. In its place, we bring our heart back into the equation of life and start asking the "questions behind the questions" while feeling our way to a new reality born of collaboration, goodwill, integrity and dignity. This is both an art and a science as we explore the depths of our love and discover vast new potentials within which to share it with the world.

The peace and love we seek to experience in our lives is unfolding as an intuitive expansion from within our individual and collective awareness. As a result, we are quickly restoring our right relationship with life. The very nature of life is to give of itself in order to expand more life. From the smallest particle to a cosmic spiral of galaxies, this exchange of energy and form plays out in a continuous rhythm in which the universe creates, evolves and recycles the building blocks of material reality. In these universal realms, energy is endlessly abundant and available to become any form, eventually returning to its native energy to be born anew in another form. Sharing is simply an aspect of creation where the whole benefits from this energetic and unconditional exchange.

Our precious earth is a living example of this exquisite and creative exchange. Whether plant, animal or mineral, each requires elements of the other to sustain and evolve life. Life also integrates elements from beyond our planet, like sunlight and electromagnetic influences for example, to ensure the maintained balance of energy to develop more life. As our orb travels through space, it too has an effect on the celestial bodies it passes by with gravitational forces that nudge and pull upon its neighbors.

We humans are equally and intrinsically a part of this same process. Our bodies come from the ingredients provided by our planet and likewise return to become potentials for another expression, another day. Our very existence relies on the precise flow and interaction of energies that is integral to this universal blueprint. Over time, we have forgotten our own role in this grand scheme of infinite potential.

We bring one unique element to creation – our conscious

awareness of love. Each of us has the ability to think and feel, imagine and manifest. Beyond even these amazing attributes, we interrelate with all the elements in a distinctive cognizant fashion by understanding that love unites it all. As we interconnect with the countless aspects of energy that make up our existence, we have the extraordinary opportunity to give of ourselves as nothing else can.

Kindness, Compassion and Collaboration

The awakening of our heart is leading us to question our methods, beliefs and long-held structures based in a dated notion of separation from all that is. A burgeoning and amazingly diverse global population, coupled with a precipitous realization of our resulting human impact upon our earth and her peoples, is compelling a dialogue and internal investigation that promises to shift our lives to their core. Through this transformative process, we are initiating an era of peace – both within ourselves and around the world.

To achieve a collective experience of local and global peace, it is imperative that we understand who we are on the deepest personal level. Without a recognition and discovery of our worth and universal nature as empowered creative beings, we are destined to remain in the illusion and false sense of separation from each other and ourselves. Self-awareness is the beginning point that propels us forward towards a peaceful global culture that is cultivated within our own being by balancing the creative expression of our heart and the practical application of our mind.

Within the past few decades, our advancing awareness of one another as fellow humans is growing exponentially, both in our own evolving consciousness and in technology, which is encouraging and amplifying this connection with one another. What was normally a focus on local levels to address the needs of our immediate community, we are suddenly expanding to a global realization that we are all one family intricately intertwined with each other and our planetary environment. Division and separation are transforming into borderless recognition of unity. Gone are the days where we could consciously declare one better than the other, or that somehow what happens around the world does not affect us personally. We are equally becoming aware of the many disruptive and detrimental qualities we are placing on our environment.

Even though this shift has been underway for some time, the recent advent of technology, advances of science, and explosion of information, have converged and accelerated our current potential. Together, they combine to reveal a vast new arena of universal oneness. It is also opening something unexpected: our collective hearts. What peace and love-based visionaries already know is finding its way into the core population - we must think with our hearts and feel with our minds if we are to evolve and endure as a race of people.

As mentioned before, we have always been a collective humanity; however, it is particularly fascinating that science and technology are igniting this outer remembering since we do not often associate science and materialism with issues of the heart. How has it managed to do this? By improving the spontaneous sharing of information, social connections and resources, which awakened us to the plight and challenges we face universally. Images, pictures, news, art, culture, language, and customs are a few of the universally and, in many cases, instantly available resources and understandings literally at our fingertips.

Collaboration is swiftly becoming the norm as it replaces the outdated competitive perspective. By recognizing our shared ability to affect positive change on an individual and group level, we are allowing the creative stimulus of collective problem solving to occur in quick form rather than stifling our progress by the competitive control of resources and ideas that has been the approach of the past. The World Wide Web, for example, conceived as a social and cultural enhancement and undertaken as a collaborative creation, allows us to utilize its benefits to connect with countless people around the globe. These collective attributes allow us to share information in real time across diverse nations and cultural divides. Individuals in distant lands are now our teachers of culture and diversity with direct, unfiltered and firsthand personal experience.

In order to create collaborative solutions to address the problems we face as individuals and society, it is necessary to be conscious of each other as our planetary brothers and sisters. We are all in this together and through helping, teaching and encouraging each other, we translate our local efforts into actions on a grand scale that incorporate a broader understanding that every choice we make is having an impact on all. A collaborative global family promises to bring a new harmony to humanity and it is our privilege to be its present-day participants and prospective architects.

The Unexpected Element - New Generations and the Social-Technology Age

To gain even greater insights to our unfolding human potential, it is important to recognize an underlying phenomenon that is unique to this particular era of time on our planet. The new generations, being born the past several decades, seem better equipped, more connected and informed than any previous time. This further clarifies how the shift of our potential is occurring so rapidly right now. Where we experienced natural shifts in previous centuries from the agrarian to industrial era, for example, nothing compares to the swift, organic and fluid shifts that are underway now.

This notable trend is mainly associated to the modern day post war-era generations and the impact of information, technology and expanded awareness of the children being born at this specific time. Not only are the most recent generations being exposed and stimulated by a substantially greater amount of information than has ever been available before, these children have near or real-time access to an almost infinite spectrum of historical, scientific, and cultural, data and ideas. Known over the past decades by a variety of social labels: Baby Boomers, Generation X, Generation Y or Millennials, and most recently, iGen or Generation Z, each subsequent generation benefits from the previous with an almost exponential growth in awareness and humanitarian understanding.

These newer generations are the inspirers and creators of advanced technology and social media, which provides for the first time, a first person account of our experience of life as part of an international public dialogue. For example, when on social sites like Facebook or Twitter, people are free to express very personal experiences and opinions live and immediately, often far beyond their original circle of friends, reaching a global audience. Corroborated or criticized in real time, this mostly uncensored and unfiltered dialogue is bringing a constant evolving kaleidoscope of beliefs, attitudes, issues, problems and ideas to our mutual awareness.

For many, the exposure to such a vast array of arts, culture, science, technology and information at large, provides a strong platform that naturally encourages unity and cooperation at levels not previously known. In the most recent period alone, we have children being born in an era of technology literally growing up with direct access to worldwide social communication, interactions and engagement with cultures and universal ideas in addition to their own.

With each of these generations expanding their knowledge base far beyond the previous group, it is easy to see that our collective awareness and potential is escalating towards a unity and collaborative approach to life. The children of today, and those of tomorrow, already have this holistic understanding as part of their consciousness. They do not adhere to former racial and ethnic divides, for example. As they come of age, they are building their organizations and structures around the wisdom that we are all part of the whole, including the environment, unlike previous generations that ignored or denigrated this realization.

Against this background of current transformative change, however, it is necessary to acknowledge that many fanatics are also making use of social media, online live broadcasts, and various other technological disruptors, to instill fear and hatred. This is often a challenge response by traditional and fundamentalist religious societies, political radicalization and violent extremism in many social forms, which has taken advantage of the same technology and social interactions to accomplish their tasks of a humiliation and intimidation nature. This is an example of the negative outgrowths of technological development where the separatist view is still predominant, and why it becomes increasingly necessary for love and understanding to overcome negative technological applications.

We Are the Change and the Solution

Fundamental change comes from a desire deep within the core of our being. It is the recognition and release of obsolete, limiting beliefs that no longer serve us while simultaneously choosing fresh, vital ideas and potentials that resonate with that deep inner vision. By acknowledging and letting go of the thoughts, perspectives, and attachments to the journeys of yesterday, through the conscious act of forgiveness and release, each of us is creating a reality based on love and peace. Together we are manifesting a new paradigm and opportunity to live in harmony.

This is the inside-out approach to living. Going within first to determine what is best for us by listening to our heart rather than reacting to life as we observe and witness it from the outside. It is time to return within and find our own voice and ideas about life. To restore our individual and collective health, wealth and well-being, we must come from our personal center and balance - our heart. From this perspective, we can base our daily decisions with inner peace, harmony, clarity and wisdom and thereby affect positive, peaceful change.

Numerous beliefs, ideas, notions, and understandings of life drive each of us, setting the tone for our personal and shared story. The challenge is that we are much more than our present story and, in most cases, our personal and global script of life is out of date and unproductive. It no longer serves us. The more we tune in to our inner realm of consciousness, the more we become aware of who we are and our infinite potential.

Although conflicts born of discrimination, humiliation and ignorance of the precious value of life may continue for a while, how we personally approach life and the choices we make alters the timing and the outcome. Accepting and loving ourselves unconditionally initiates our expanding conscious awareness of the boundless beauty in life. As we embrace one another as fellow humans, we dissolve age-old conflicts and restore the dignity and diversity that is both our heritage and our destiny. Simply be a friend first.

Bibliography

Anderson, Royce. "A definition of peace." Peace and Conflict: *Journal of Peace Psychology* 10.2 (2004): 101.

Becker, Harold W. *Internal Power - Seven Doorways to Self-Discovery.* Tampa: White Fire Tampa, FL 2008.

Becker, Harold W. *Unconditional Love – An Unlimited Way of Being, White Fire*, Tampa, FL 2007.

Braden, Gregg. *The Turning Point*, Hay House, 2014.

Davidson, William L. "Definition of Consciousness." in *Mind* 23 (1881): 406-412.

Hanh, Thich Nhat. *Peace is every step: The path of mindfulness in everyday life.* Bantam, 1991.

Lindner, Evelyn, *Making Enemies: Humiliation and International*

Conflict, Praeger Publishers, 2006.

Lindner, Evelyn, *Honor, Humiliation, and Terror: An Explosive Mix – And How We Can Defuse It with Dignity*, World Dignity University Press, 2017

MacKenzie, Donald, and Judy Wajcman. T*he social shaping of technology*. Open University press, 1999.

Ray, Paul H, and Sherry Ruth Anderson. *The Cultural Creatives*, Harmony Books, 2000.

Ray, Sondra. *Loving Relationships*, Celestial Arts, Berkeley, CA 1995.

Smith, Huston. *The Religions of Man*, Harper Perennial, New York, NY 1989.

Starr, Jerold M. "The peace and love generation: Changing attitudes toward sex and violence among college youth." In *Journal of Social Issues* 30.2 (1974): 73-106.

Zemke, Ron, Claire Raines, and Bob Filipczak. *Generations at work: Managing the clash of Veterans, Boomers, Xers, and Nexters in your workplace.* New York, NY: Amacom, 2000.

MYTH VALUES: AN APPROACH TO UNDERSTANDING ETHNIC CONFLICTS

Muli wa Kyendo

The World of Mythology

Ethnic conflict is likely to occur when members of cultures with substantially different myth values come into contact with one another

When the first secondary school with students from various ethnic groups opened in Kenya in 1926, hopes were high that the country had started on a journey to create lasting harmony among the various unrelated and hitherto unfamiliar communities coerced to live together as a nation by the British colonial rule. The idea behind the project was that more contact among students belonging to different ethnic groups would weaken negative stereotypes the students may have had of each other and consequently reduce their mutual antipathies. The students were expected to diffuse the positive experiences to their communities through their changed attitudes and behaviors. This however, didn't happen. A recent study by the National Cohesion and Integration Commission of Kenya showed that most Kenyans would still not trust anyone who is not from their own ethnic groups. Indeed, in 2008, ethnic conflicts flared up bringing the country to the brink of a catastrophe similar to that which occurred in Rwanda in 1994. More contact and increased multiethnic schools did not reduce the potential of ethnic conflict. Despite the failure however, the thinking underlying the project, now known as the "contact hypothesis", is still influential in Kenyan policy making circles.

In his book, *Theories of Conflict*, Johan Galtung (1958), stresses the importance of attitudes and behavior in conflict. But he also says attitudes and behavior come from what he calls, "implicit cultural elements" or "standards" acquired from the social system. In this analysis I will rename "implicit cultural elements" and "standards" as "values and attitudes" which are acquired from the social system through myths, legends and folktales which, in turn, I will together refer to as "myth values". My argument is that ethnic conflict is likely to occur when members of cultures with substantially different myth values come into contact with one another.

Myth values clothe themselves in human rituals, ceremonies, song, dance and religion among other customs. They are deeply entrenched in human psyche directing the way we view the world. They have the ability to twist and turn to accommodate new realities and circumstances. Arthur Frank (2010), a leading folklorist, states, "Stories work with people, for people, and always stories work on people, affecting what people are able to see as real, as possible, and as worth doing or best avoided."

To argue my case, I will focus on Kenya where in 2008, as I have already stated, a post-election ethnic violence brought the country to the brink of massacre in a scale similar to that of the Rwandan genocide of 1994. Thousands of Kenyans were brutally murdered or maimed while thousands of others were injured or left homeless. Although the conflict was resolved by the concerted effort of the international community led by the former UN Secretary General Dr. Kofi Annan, Kenyans — like many other Africans in the continent — have continued to live in fear of ethnic conflicts breaking out with more disastrous consequences. In deed, the situation can only be described as a truce or what experts euphemistically refer to as "silent conflict".

Let me pause at this point to briefly explain my understanding of the key concepts that form the basis of my argument, demonstrating how they relate to the discussion.

Key Concepts

Values

Values have traditionally been regarded as core aspects of the self-concept and as such a form of 'basic truths' about the reality. Gabriel E. Dang (2015) writes, "A value can be seen as some point of view or conviction which we can live with, live by and can even *die for*" (emphasis is mine). In all cultures, values are part of the heritage that is passed down from one generation to another.

Attitudes

Attitudes are the response or behavior that is a result of our values. Attitudes thus develop as a result of evaluative responding (for example, approval or disapproval, favor or disfavor, liking or disliking, approach or avoidance, attraction or aversion), which produces a psychological tendency to respond with a particular degree of evaluation when encountering the attitude object. While values are more or less permanent, attitudes are changeable with favorable experiences.

Values and attitudes are the forces behind intentions and behavior.

Myth, Legend and Folktale

The terms legend and folktale are sometimes used interchangeably with myth. Looking at their origins and purposes however, these are not the same. Donna Rosenberg (1997), in her book, *Folklore, Myth, and Legends: A World Perspective* offers some useful guidelines to distinguish the three, which I shall adopt for this discussion.

A *myth* is a sacred story from the past. It may explain the origin of the universe and of life, or it may express its culture's moral values in human terms. Myths concern the powers that control the human world and the relationship between those powers and human beings.

A *legend* is a story from the past about a subject that was, or is believed to have been, historical. Legends concern people, places, and events. Usually, the subject is a saint, a king, a hero, a famous person, or a war. A legend is always associated with a particular place and a particular time in history.

A *folktale* is a story that, in its plot, is pure fiction and that has no particular location in either time or space. However, despite its elements of fantasy, a folktale is actually a symbolic way of presenting the different means by which human beings cope with the world in which they live. Folktales concern people, either royalty or common folk, or animals who speak and act like people.

Culture

In this discussion, the word "culture" is used to refer to the tangible or visible manifestation of the values and attitudes — myth values— which are spread within a community through myths, legends and folktales. Culture entails a totality of traits that are peculiar to a people to the extent that it marks them out from other peoples or societies. These peculiar traits include shared values and assumptions that the people or a community acquires over generations. Shared values are myth values that form the basis of assumptions a community uses to establish and reinforce the attitudes that the people use to judge what appropriate behavior is in a particular situation or setting. Myth values constitute the directional force behind human behavior, which creates physical artifacts, social institutions, cultural symbols and rituals.

Origin and Functions of Myths, Legends and Folktales

With this in mind, we can now discuss the origin and functions of myths, legends and folktales. According to Mircea Eliade (1963) myths often develop to justify the current state of affairs. In traditional cultures, the entities and forces described in myths of origin are often considered sacred. Thus, by attributing the state of the universe to the actions of these entities and forces, myths of origin give the current order an aura of sacredness.

Others who hold similar views include the Tunisian historian Ibn Khaldun ((1332 – 1406). Writing on how human civilization develops, Khaldun sees myths, legends and folktale as originating in the need for social control when people come together to form communities. Human organization necessitates the selection of a person with power and authority over others. Such a person is shrouding in myths to generate unquestioned obedience from others. Ruling monarchs or aristocracies may allege descent from mythical founders, gods or heroes in order to legitimize their control.

These descriptions of the origin of myths are indicative of the problem that we are faced with when trying to understand the influence of myths, legends and folktales on human beings. The idea that myths, legends and folktales validate rather than establish conditions of living is widely held and of long standing. It is the reason why they have been largely ignored as originators of behavior when searching for solutions to human problems. However the Bible and other ancient writings, contain many instances where myths and legends originate or precede reality. Kebra Nagast, the ancient holy book of Ethiopia, says that God in making Adam placed in body of Adam a "pearl" which passes into the bodies of holy men and others of great human achievement.

The pearl, according to Kebra Nagast, entered into the body of the King Solomon through David. The pearl, some Ethiopian priests argue, entered into the body of Virgin Mary resulting in the birth of Jesus Christ. Similar beliefs are shared by many African communities who believe that life comes from external sources (generally spirits) and that the sources determine human character and behavior (compare with genes). A biblical example is the story of Abraham and the myth of a "select land" given to him by God for his children. The Bible says that following the vision (a conversation with his god in a dream) Abraham left Ur and migrated to Canaan to become "the father of a multitude of nations" in a new land (Genesis 17:5).

This myth, planted by forces outside human beings (god of Abraham), established the roots for the action (moving to the "promised land") and spurned a legend that today defines three major, antagonistic "Abrahamic" religions in the world (Judaism, Christianity, and Islam). This view would hardly have surprised Alfred Russel Wallance, one of the world's greatest scientists and the co-discoverer (with Charles Darwin) of the theory of evolution who "felt that some metaphysical force" had directed evolution of human consciousness (Jaynes,1982). In deed, Wallance spent most of his later life seeking " the origin of man's intellectual and moral nature in man's nonhuman ancestors (Kottler, 1974).

In this analysis I take the view of these ancient thinkers to show that myths, legends and folktales initiate reality and create conditions of living for human beings and that through the myth values they carry, they can determine whether we live in peace or war.

Review of current theories of ethnic conflict
Increasing ethnic and racial conflicts – especially in Africa - have led to an increase in explanations of the causes. Most of the explanations take their cue from Marxist dialectical materialism,

a labor-based theory of wealth, an economic class struggle leading to revolution, the dictatorship of the proletariat, and the eventual development of a classless society. These explanations assume that development is a precondition for peaceful interethnic relations.

Opposing theories support capitalism with the argument that as countries develop along the capitalist Western path, ethnic identities will progressively become politically unimportant. They will be replaced by national affiliations and identities which will make ethnic tensions and violent conflicts a thing of the past.

Critics of both Marxist and capitalist theories point to the resurgence of ethnic conflicts in Eastern Europe which have intensified fears of similar resurges in the rest of Europe. What is surprising is that the emerging ethnic disputes in Eastern Europe appear much as they were when they were suppressed by Soviet power many years ago. As I.S. Griffiths (1993) describes the situation, "It is almost as though we had simply turned back the clock or, to change the analogy, as though they were the patients described by Oliver Sacks who came back to life after medication had released them from the strange disease that had frozen them". The catastrophe may not have occurred yet, but it is obvious that the notions that "modernity" would result in a utopian classless society or a smooth transition from Gemeinschaft (community with strong kinship ties) to Gesellschaft (association, detached from ethnic sentiments), with gradual dissolution of ethnic affiliations, simply have not worked.

Another important group – the primordialists - put the cause of ethnic clashes on primordial attachments which apparently make ethnic conflicts inevitable in modern societies. The argument is that "ethnic groups and nationalities exist because there are traditions of belief and action towards primordial objects such as biological features and especially territorial location". Steven Grosby (1994), relying on the assumptions of strong ties of kinship among members of ethnic groups, argues that this kinship "makes it possible for ethnic groups to think in terms of family resemblances". Clifford Geertz (1993) asserts that ethnic groups will always threaten the survival of civil governments but not the existence of nations formed by one ethnic group. Ethnic wars in countries such as Yugoslavia, Rwanda and the Democratic Republic of Congo are cited as good examples.

Critics have however, pointed out that this theory tends to emphasize the irrationality of ethnic violence and leans towards an idea of genetically induced barbaric behavior projecting a picture of hopelessness and perceiving ethnic conflict as permanent and ineradicable.

Similarly, elite manipulation theories which stress the role of political leaders and their ability to incite masses to violence have been criticized for assuming people do not have the ability to make rational choices and for not explaining why leaders so easily exhort obedience. The argument of the elite manipulation theories is that political leaders who lose legitimacy in the eyes of the people appeal to their ethnic groups to secure their stay at power. Through the mass media, over which they have privileged control, they achieve mobilization of their people around a nationalist goal and thus "construct" ethnic conflict.

The failure of these theories and explanations to translate into meaningful peace has led to the call for a shift in thinking — for "profound, radical, and sustainable transformation" — transformation that will fundamentally alter the very nature of "our vision and perception". As one commentator put it, the task requires courage to challenge basic assumptions and lifelong traditions. It demands boldness to place major bets on new ideas, models, and strategies. The theory of myth values aims to make such a contribution by examining myth values and their role in promoting ethnic peace or conflict.

MYTH VALUES THEORY
An Analysis of Values and Attitudes of Myths and Legends for Ethnic Harmony.

INTRODUCTION
Although, so far, I have talked of myths, legends and folktales, I will concentrate on myths and legends for the purpose of this analysis. True, folktales speak to universal and timeless themes but it is also true that they have functions other than those identified for myths and legends (Rosenberg, 1997). More importantly also, unlike myths and legends, folktales carry universal human values and are, possibly for this reason, generally dispersed across communities, nations and continents, often taking on the characteristics of the time and place in which they are retold. W. W. Newell (1895) in his article "Theories of Diffusion of Folktales", was of the view that each folktale has a single origin from which it has spread to all parts of the earth where conditions allowed exchange, mingled with the stock already present, and modified in ways now untraceable. A good example are Aesop's fables which have spread around the world making them a part of human heritage. On the other hand, myths and legends carry community values and are culture and place specific (Rosenberg, 1997). In the society in which they are told, they are regarded as conveying profound truths, metaphorically, symbolically and even in a historical or literal sense.

THE APPROACH
Choice of Case Studies
Kenya was ruled by Britain since 1895. The British rule brought together 42 ethnic groups, many of which were not only unfamiliar with each other but also had different myth values. The country won its independence in 1963 as one nation.

Myths and legends for this study were purposefully taken from four ethnic groups — Luo, Kalenjin, Kikuyu and Kamba. Three of them — Kikuyu, Luo and Kalenjin— were selected because they are the main protagonists in ethnic conflicts in the country. The Kamba were chosen because their region has been described as a "haven of peace" (Baldauf, 2008; Spencer, 1972; Gadsden, 1974).

Approach to Myth and Legend Text Analysis

I will proceed to analyze the myths and legends by isolating the themes. Analyzing themes in texts or narratives is regarded by most scholars as highly indicative of the essential personality of a culture. Such analysis allows us to talk about values, beliefs and other orientations collectively known as "cultural patterns". Researchers, such as Richard Porter and Edwin McDaniel (2007), define cultural patterns as "a system of beliefs and values that work in combination to provide a coherent, if not always consistent, model for perceiving the world."

For elaboration and clarity purposes, I will also use paratextual elements. Gerald Genette (1997) describes paratextual elements as all messages which are situated, at least originally, outside the text such as media interviews and conversations, or under the cover of private communication such as correspondence and private journals. In other words, I will use other written materials which have a bearing on my analysis.

I will then analyze the ethnic groups' reactions to colonial experiences in relation to their myth values before proceeding to analyze the groups' reaction to modern nationhood. Colonial experience is the most traumatic event that affected all ethnic groups that came to form the country we now call Kenya. As Sharif Kanaana (1994) says with reference to the Palestinian situation, colonial occupation threatens the identities of ethnic groups which are moved to come together to re-affirm their "unified heritage and to have shared symbols, which will preserve their union like one cohesive nation (ethnic group) more than any time before". The purpose here is to demonstrate how the communities' myth values shaped the selected ethnic groups' reactions to colonialism and how they continue to shape ethnic relations in independent Kenya.

My overall effort is to argue that ethnic and racial conflict is likely to occur when members of cultures with substantially different myth values come into contact with one another.

THE ANALYSIS
Kikuyu

The Kikuyu story is legend about a man named Gikuyu. Gikuyu meets Ngai (God) who takes him to the top of Kirinyaga,(Mt. Kenya) from where he gives him "a share of his land with rivers, valleys, forests rich with fruits and animals of all types". Ngai points out a place (Mukurwe wa Gathanga) where Gikuyu and his wife named Mumbi would put up their home. Gikuyu and Mumbi get nine daughters but no sons. Gikuyu goes back to Ngai and says that he needs sons to marry his daughters. Ngai tells him:

> Go, take a lamb and a kid. Kill these under the big mugumo tree near the homestead and take the blood and the fat. Pour them on the trunk of the tree. Let the family make a big fire under the tree. The meat will burn as a sacrifice. When you take your wife and daughters home, go back alone to the mugumo tree. There you will find nine very handsome men who are willing to marry your daughters.

The legend ends with a commandment from Ngai for the Kikuyu people to "increase and multiply and fill all the land."

(Source of legend: Kenyatta, J.,1966, *My People of Kikuyu*, Oxford University Press, Nairobi).

Key Themes

- Land theme dominates (establishment of a settlement a homestead as opposed to a family. Ngai tells Gikuyu, "Go build a homestead") This is also emphasized in the ending.

- Establishment of a people – the Kikuyu - in a named place and time

- Establishment of an archetypical family, Gikuyu and Mumbi.

- Establishment of worship (culture)

Myth values

- You are less than a Kikuyu if you don't own land to establish a homestead

- Achievement comes from of Ngai through the ancestors Gikuyu and Mumbi.

- To maintain and practice Kikuyu culture entitles a member to benefit from Ngai through Gikuyu and Mumbi.

Kamba

The Kamba story is a myth about how the human race was established on earth. The myth says that in the beginning Mulungu (God) created first man and his wife in spirit form just like him. He dropped them from heaven to earth, together with their cattle, a stool, the Kiikamba language and everything else they needed. They landed on the mountain of Nzaui (possibly a mythological mountain).

The man and his wife bore only boys, so they prayed to God for girls to marry their sons. God caused rain to fall down on earth forming anthills. God then came down to earth, took clay from the anthills and made another set of human beings - a man and a woman. The first man and his wife became the Clan of Spirits and the second man and his wife became the Clan of Clay. The Clan of Clay had beautiful daughters who married the sons of Clan of Spirits and they gave as dowry the cattle that Mulungu gave them.

The Kamba myth ends with dispersal of human beings after they forgot to sacrifice to Mulungu.

Mulungu dispersed them and increased languages. Some of the people became Maasai speaking Maasai language, others became Kikuyu and spoke Kikuyu and so all communities on earth were formed with their languages. The Akamba were left with the original language – Kiikamba - that Mulungu gave human beings.

(Source of myth: Ndeti, K. 1972, *Elements of Akamba Life*, East African Publishing House, Nairobi.)

Key Themes
- Establishment of a human race on earth
- Establishment of a human family (parents and children)
- Establishment of human relations as indicated by the detail about dowry and language. It is noteworthy that the dowry was established by Mulungu.
- Establishment of worship (culture)
- Establishes the oneness of human race. This theme is emphasized in the ending.

Key values
- Human being are brothers and sisters, with the Kamba being the first born
- You are subhuman if you don't have a family and in-laws
- Tolerance for "otherness" because they, too, are Kambas with different languages

Kalenjin
The Kalenjin story is about of the ethnic groups' migration in search of productive land. According to the legend, the Myoot — maternal ancestors — fled out southwards in search of a fertile land from a land of giants (sometimes referred to as Egypt) where they were oppressed.

After a long journey, they came upon a Mt. Psigiis. Standing on the mountain, the elders were impressed by the fertile land below which they made the home of the Kalenjin community. Because, during the wandering, the Kalenjin had no time to circumcise their boys, the whole Kalenjin community was forced to camp at a place called Tulwaap Monyiis for a mass circumcision ritual.

The legend ends with the establishment of circumcision rites . An affirmation reminds initiates to respect the elders and protect their land.

Our land in Kutoi
One old man said:
"Don't let it go!"

(Source of legend: Fish, B.C and Fish G.W. 1995, *The Kalenjin Heritage: Traditional Religious and Social Practices*, Africa Gospel Church).

Key themes

- Search for fertile land
- Gratitude to elders for fertile land
- Desire for freedom. They had fled from a tyrannical rule
- Establishment of community ritual of circumcision as commutity remembrance of elders. This theme is emphasized in the affirmation.

Key values

- Through their ancestors, Kaleljins are blessed because they inherited fertile land
- Land, the greatest possession, should be protected from all intruders
- Unity is important for all Kalenjins. Community circumcision rituals emphasize unity of Kalenjin, is also a reminder of the ancestors.

Luo

The legend talks about their migration to the country now called Kenya looking for a place with abundant fish. They came in waves from the north (possibly Sudan) following the River Nile.

> Those that went further afield (and reached present day Kenya) were the Joka Jok and Joka Owiny. Historian Prof. Bethwel Ogot (2009) writes that they passed through desirable lands such as Uganda, before they came upon a great lake with a lot of fish and settled by its shores. There was no unity among them, only apparently a bunch of people with one language travelling together. Without weapons and being fragmented, the Luo valued integration with the communities they found. It can also be deduced from this that reciprocal loyalty to friends was highly valued.

The Luo legend ends with them living in harmony with the people they found. Ogot writes:

> They established trade with the communities they found. This led to reciprocal borrowing of cultural ideas. For example, the Luos, who now took to farming, lost the importance they placed on cattle. And perhaps because of this, there were no efforts to change each other's culture. The Luo continued to be one of the few communities in Kenya that do not practice circumcision on both boys and girls.

(Source of legend: Ogot B. A, 2009, A *History of the Luo-Speaking Peoples of East Africa*. Kisumu, Anyange Press)

Key themes
- Search for abundant food – especially fish
- Independence (individuals did not arrive as a group)
- Reciprocal friendship. Mutually beneficial trade relations established with other communities. This theme runs throughout the narrative as reported by Prof. Ogot.
- Faith and tenacity. They followed the river believing they would find what they wanted—eventually. There is no reference to supernatural intervention.

Key values
- Luos value reciprocal friendship and loyalty
- They value non-interference with other people. They neither want to change other people, nor do they change themselves. They carried on with their non-circumcision of either boys or girls.
- Achievement is a result of individual efforts and useful relations
-Tenacity

Reaction to Colonialism

Among the Kikuyu, the name Mumbi from the Kikuyu legend was invoked as a rallying call to unite the Kikuyu in a fight against the colonialists. According to Emmanuel Akyeampong (2011),

With modern publishing facilities, the message of the legend was embellished, amplified and spread. Gakaara wa Wanjau, one of the earliest writers and publishers, published and distributed what he called the "Gikuyu and Mumbi Creed", for which the colonial government put him in detention till 1960. Parallel to that, several song books were published under the name of Gikuyu and Mumbi.

The Luos on the other had cooperated with the Whites which is consistent with their values. Ogot writes,

The Luo, who form the majority of the inhabitants of Central Nyanza, offered no armed resistance to the newcomers. The coming of marvelous 'red strangers', who were supposed to emerge from the sea, had been foretold, and the people were advised (by the seers) against showing any hostility to the intruders lest they incur the wrath of the ancestors. Hence, the Luo people welcomed the Europeans cordially, cooperated with the administration in all possible ways, and generally expected great things of the Whiteman.

Kalenjin resistance to colonial rule is well documented. Indeed, according to some records, both the Nandi and the Kipsigis, the two large communities of the Kalenjin staged concerted resistance with the Nandi resistance going down in history as the longest and most tenacious (Matson 1972).

The Kamba reaction to colonialism has been described as widespread but mostly "non-violent". As early as 1911 a movement of total European rejection had emerged which "preached radical anti-European messages.

By the 1930s, resistance had become more focused, and saw the formation of the Ukamba Members Association (UMA), one of whose leaders was Muindi Mbingu who became a hero in the struggle for independence.

Reaction to Modern State

I have already hinted to the reaction of each ethnic group analyzed to modern state. The Kikuyu and the Kalenjin myth values center on land. Conflict would therefore be expected to centre on such issues as well. Kikuyus want more "increase to fill the land" and the Kalenjins want to preserve their land, "Our land in Kutoi, One old man said: 'Don't let it go!'". The kalenjins had wedged a bitter, prolonged war on Whites to protect their land. The Luo-Kikuyu conflict is again a reflection of the myth values. Reciprocal loyalty is what Luos look for and for this reason, they have surprised other communities when they have often supported Kikuyu presidency. The Kikuyus on the other hand are deeply rooted in the myth values. They cannot get out of their archetypical family values of the House of Mumbi and the culture that supports it such as circumcision –which the Luos do not practice. The kikuyu therefore have never reciprocated by supporting a Luo presidency, a betrayal that goes against Luo myth values. The Kambas face similar conditions as those faced by the Kalenjin, the Luo and the Kikuyu in Kenya, yet their reaction has been consistent – peaceful.

CONCLUSIONS

From this analysis, we have seen that myth values direct

human beings, deciding their reaction to the major issues they face. The problem is that human beings are not aware, and with modern ideologies, it is difficult to accept that their reactions are dictated by myths and legends. Conflicts emanating from myth values can be difficult to solve as witnessed by the deadly and prolonged conflict between Christians and Muslims. The true causes have been shrouded in meaningless ideologies, making the war endless. The Kikuyu- Kalenjin conflict is very similar, with potential for protracted conflicts and uneasiness that can paralyze Kenya as a nation. We can conclude that communities with myth values based on legends with named archetypical characters, such as Gikuyu and Mumbi are more likely to initiate aggressiveness (compare with the Christian and Muslim conflicts and the legend of archetypical Abraham).

Groupthink is a group communication process where high cohesiveness of the group - in our case, ethnic group - impairs individual decision making, even when the individual is sacrificing personal or country's benefits. It characterizes communities with legends that establish archetypical founding families. As we have seen, legends are presented as historical facts and group members actually believe that the events narrated are true and that evils predicted in case of disobedience can occur. Conflict is therefore; build into the legends whenever members come into contact with others that have different myth values and therefore different cultural practices.

Founding ancestors, as in the case of the Kalenjin, may produce high collective remembrance (as in Kalenjin, initiation rites and affirmations, which remind the community of their ancestors), but not very strong groupthink. Similarly, we may say that ethnic group's legends that don't establish worship such as that of the Luos are likely to be peaceful, all other things remaining equal. Creation stories such as that of the Kamba promote oneness of humanity. With a broad-based creation story, "how human beings came on earth", creation myth values are all inclusive. Peace emanates from treating others as brothers and sisters. That is possible where myth values talk of common origin of humanity.

Modern states such as Kenya, offer excellent platforms for myth values to engage in perpetual conflict supporting our argument that ethnic conflict is likely to occur when members of cultures with substantially different myth values come into contact with one another. Conflict may be physically manifested, as for example, in the case of Kikuyu vs the Luo or Kikuyu vs Kalenjin or it might be silent as when one community takes all the key jobs or concentrates development in their region.

Silent myth value conflicts have their manifestation. We see their effect in physical manifestations such as clothing, street names, statues and memorials which demonstrate the aspects of a nation's myths and legends that are being promoted for preservation and celebration. School texts may include hero legends, songs, rhymes, fables and anecdotes from the nation's ethnic groups or from one of them. All these are signs of potential for peace or conflict. The questions to ask are: What are the messages in this body of work? Which community's myth or legend are we telling? And what potential does this hold for ethnic and racial peace or conflict?

Hope for peace in multi ethnic and multi-racial societies lies in creating all inclusive "master" stories—stories in which all communities see themselves while allowing different communities to grow and preserve their cultures. Myth values may not change – as shown by the Luos and circumcision, but attitudes and behavior can change as we have also seen.

Acknowledgement

An earlier version of this chapter was published with the title "Interethnic Conflicts: Understanding the Important Role of Folktales" in *Handbook of Research on Examining Global Peacemaking in the Digital Age* by Bruce L. Cook (editor). I am grateful to Prof. John S. Mbiti who read that version in draft form and made very useful corrections and comments, most of which were unfortunately not implemented due to time and space restrictions but which have now been incorporated. I am also indebted to him for his encouragement. Prof. Mbiti is the author of the classic book, *African Religions and Philosophy* which is "a systematic study of the attitudes of mind and belief that have evolved in the many societies of Africa". I am also indebted to Prof. Bruce L. Cook for painstakingly editing the earlier version of this Chapter.

References

Akyeampong E K. and Gates H. L. (Eds) *Dictionary of African Biography*, Oxford University Press, 2011

Baldauf, S., How can Kenya avoid ethnic war? *Christian Science Monitor*, January 30, 2008

Barrette T., Imagination, The Hamitic Myth And Rwanda: The Foundation Of Division In Rwanda, M. A Thesis Faculty of California State University, Fullerton, 2016

Chukwu Dan O., Racism, Hamitic Hypothesis And African Theories Of Origin: The Unending Debate? *Journal of Integrative Humanism*, 2014

Edith R. Sanders, The Hamitic Hypothesis; Its Origin and Functions in Time Perspective. *Journal of African History*, 1969

Eliade Mircea, Myth and Reality,Harper (1963)

Everett, Jim A. C., Intergroup Contact Theory: Past, Present, and Future. *The Inquisitive Mind* magazine, Issue 2, 2013

Frank A., Letting Stories Breathe: A Socio-Narratology, 2010

Fish Burnette C and Fish Gerald W. *The Kalenjin Heritage: Traditional Religious and Social Practices*, 1995

Geert Hofstede, *Cultures and Organizations: Software of the Mind*, 2010

Genette, G. (1997). *Paratexts: Thresholds of interpretation* (J. E. Lewin, Trans.). New York: Cambridge University Press

Gadsden, Fay. Further Notes on the Kamba Destocking

Controversy of 1938. *The International Journal of African Historical Studies,* Vol. 7, No. 4 (1974)

Griffiths S. I, Nationalism and Ethnic Conflict Threats to European Security. *SIPRI Research Report* No. 5 Oxford University Press, 1993

Gryosby S., The verdict of history: The inexpugnable tie of primordiality hutch – A response to Eller and Coughlan. *Ethnic and Racial Studies* 17(1), pp. 164-171, 1994

ibn Khaldun, *The Muqaddimah* (translated by Franz Rosenthal) , 1998

Idang Gabriel E., African Culture and values. *Phronimon,* Volume 16, Number 2 2015

Johnson, Jeannie and Berrett, Matthew, Cultural Topography: A New Research Tool for Intelligence Analysis. *Studies in Intelligence.* Vol. 55, No. 2 (2011)

Jaynes, J. *The origin of Consciousness in the Breakdown of the Bicameral Mind,* Houghton Mifflin Company, 1982

Johan Galtung, *Theories of Conflict,* Colombia University, 1958

Kanaana, Sharif Folk Heritage of Palestine, Tayibeh, *Israel: Research Centre for Arab Heritage,* (1994).

Kenyatta, J.,1966, *My People of Kikuyu,* Oxford University Press, Nairobi.

Kottler,M. J (1974), Alfred Russel Wallace, The Origin of Man, and Spiritualism, *Isis,* Vol. 65, No. 2

Lugan Bernard, *African Legacy: Solutions for a Community in Crisis,* Carnot USA Books, 2004

Matson, A.T *Nandi Resistance to British Rule 1890–190.* East African Publishing House, 1972.

Moritz Merker, *Die Masai: Ethnographische Monographie eines ostafrikanischen Semitenvolkes,* 1904.

Murdock G. P., (1959) *Africa, Its Peoples and Their Culture History* ,New York, .

Newell W.W. "Theories of Diffusion of Folk-Tales", *The Journal of American Folklore,* Vol. 8, No. 28 (Jan. - Mar., 1895),

Ogot B. A (2009) *A History of the Luo-Speaking Peoples of East Africa.* Kisumu: Anyange Press

Rosenberg D., *Folklore, Myths, and Legends : A World Perspective,* 1997.

Venkatasawmy R Ethnic Conflict in Africa: A Short Critical Discussion. *Transience Vol. 6,* Issue 2, 2015.